How to Improve Your Chess

How to Improve Your Chess

Your Chess

by I. A. Horowitz
Three-time U.S. Open Champion

AND

Fred Reinfeld

Collier Books
Macmillan Publishing Company
New York

Collier Macmillan Publishers
London

Macmillan Publishing Company
866 Third Avenue, New York, N.Y. 10022
Collier Macmillan Canada, Inc.

Library of Congress Cataloging-in-Publication Data
Horowitz, I. A. (Israel Albert), 1907-1973.
    How to improve your chess.
    Originally published: New York : Dutton, 1952.
    Includes index.
    1. Chess—Middle games.   I. Reinfeld, Fred,
1910-1964.   II. Title.
GV1450.3.H6   1986   794.1'23   86-9705
ISBN 0-02-028890-5

First Collier Books Edition 1972

18 19 20 21 22 23 24 25 26 27

How to Improve Your Chess was published in a
hardcover edition by Harvey House, Publishers,
and is reprinted by arrangement with I. A.
Horowitz and the estate of Fred Reinfeld.

Macmillan books are available at special discounts
for bulk purchases for sales promotions, premiums,
fund-raising, or educational use. For details, contact:

Special Sales Director
Macmillan Publishing Company
866 Third Avenue
New York, N.Y. 10022

Printed in the United States of America

Introduction

THE other day a group of boys were having a snowball fight. When a toddler appeared on the scene, one of the older boys began to pelt him.

"Why are you hitting me?" the child sobbed. "I'm not hitting you!"

"Who cares?" his tormentor shouted back. "You're dere!"

The chessplayer who is not competitively equipped is pretty much in the position of that little boy. Chess is a highly competitive game, and the player who lags behind in strength—playing strength—loses out in results, and in enjoyment as well.

The present volume is intended not for outright beginners, but for intermediate players—those who have learned the rudiments of the game at one time or another. They would like to improve their play, but have not had, and do not have, the time for intensive and prolonged study. When they examine the available chess literature, they find that most books do not quite meet their particular needs. Many of the books are intended for those who are just about to become chessplayers; other books are suitable only for readers who have attained to a very fair degree of playing skill.

This book, then, is frankly addressed to the thousands of readers who play chess and feel the need for improvement without being in a position to devote too much time and effort to that improvement. The study of master games is not likely to be of much help to this type of player. The masterpieces are too refined, too rarefied for the average player, and abound in a myriad of subtle details which never appear in his own games.

In this book, however, the reader will find only games admirably suited to his needs. *For these games were played by average players—players like himself.* The games used by us were carefully sifted from hundreds of such scores, with a view to discovering the themes which are most likely to be useful to the type of reader we have had in mind. In these down-to-earth contests you will find blunders, inconsistencies, missed opportunities, faulty planning, or no planning at all—just as you encounter them in your own games.

These negative features are pointed out, described and analyzed; their consequences are made clear. The reader is shown *typical* mistakes, and how and why to avoid them.

But the negative approach is not enough! The average player moves on impulse, or merely because it is his turn to play. His great over-all failing is his inability to plan, to foresee, to build up a position with certain desired characteristics. The ability to conceive a given kind of position and then bring it into being is the most creative aspect of chess, and offers the deepest satisfaction that you can derive from the game. On the other hand, the player who cannot formulate plans is bound to be unhappy; sometimes he is discontented about the state of his chessplaying without being aware of the precise cause of his dissatisfaction.

We have not tried to teach the reader all that can be known about chess!—nobody is in a position to do that. But we have tried to impart certain attitudes, an awareness of basic problems, a familiarity with methods and techniques which have proved helpful to many students. And so we believe that any average chessplayer who reads this book will benefit considerably in greater skill and understanding, and consequently in enjoyment of "the royal game."

To the extent that our efforts have been successful, we wish to express our thanks for the courteous co-operation of the Publishers, particularly Messrs. Elliott Macrae, George Acklom and B. D. Recca.

New York,
March 1, 1952

Contents

PART I

Problems of Tactical Play

I

Be Vigilant to Seize Capturing Opportunities

THE NUMBER of capturing opportunities overlooked by the average player is really staggering. When a master gives a simultaneous exhibition against anywhere from twenty to sixty opponents, he has something like half a minute for each move he makes. Yet his percentage of oversights is relatively slight: he has a professional "batting eye." Constant practice makes him alert, and almost without looking, he sees threats, captures, checks and counterattacks.

It is easy—and thoughtless—to credit this alertness to genius. The alertness is derived from steady, grueling practice and study. Most of us lack the time for such intensive training, but it helps considerably to be aware of the problem and to be determined to root out this basic flaw in your playing ability.

RUY LOPEZ

White	Black
1. P—K 4	P—K 4

The virtues of opening the game with a center Pawn move are well known.

Open lines are immediately created for two pieces (King Bishop and Queen). Castling is facilitated by the development of the King Bishop. Furthermore, each player exercises control of the squares Q 5 and K B 5.

Repeatedly, in the course of reading this book, you will observe the importance of the center area. It could be explained here on theoretical grounds, but the explanation will be more effective if it is made piecemeal in relation to specific moves and situations.

2.   Kt—K B 3   ... ...

White develops his King Knight aggressively. "Developing" your pieces simply means: getting them into action. And the Knight develops aggressively, for Black's King Pawn is attacked.

Now that the King Knight is out, White is a step nearer to castling.

2.   ... ...   Kt—Q B 3

Black develops his Queen Knight, simultaneously defending his attacked King Pawn.

(A Knight or Bishop is worth at least three Pawns in the opening stage; hence it would be foolish for White to give up his King Knight for Black's King Pawn.)

3.   B—Kt 5   ... ...

This is the characteristic position of the Ruy Lopez, one of the most important of all the chess openings.

Diagram 1

Standard Ruy Lopez position

(Note, by the way, that with his King Knight and Bishop developed, White is ready to castle on the Kingside. This will assure the safety of his King and also prepare to get his King Rook into active play.)

By developing his Bishop, White threatens to capture the Knight (the protector of Black's King Pawn), and then play Kt × P.

3. ... ...   P—Q R 3

The threat turns out to be only a sham threat. For if 4 B × Kt, QP × B; 5 Kt × P, White's win of a Pawn is only transient. Black recovers the lost Pawn immediately, either by 5 ... Q—Kt 4 (attacking White's Knight and King Knight Pawn) or 5 ... Q—Q 5 (attacking White's Knight and his King Pawn).

4. B—R 4   ... ...

White retreats his Bishop, as he feels (rightly) that this piece still has many opportunities for usefulness.

In addition, modern players have the feeling that the

Bishop is *slightly* more valuable than the Knight, and hence the exchange B × Kt is avoided unless some specially good reason presents itself.

> **4.** ... ...   **Kt—B 3**

As Black does not fear the "threat" to his King Pawn, he counterattacks against White's King Pawn. This (like White's second move) is a good move. Black develops with counterattack.

> **5. Q—K 2**   ... ...

White makes still another developing move to guard his King Pawn.

As a rule, the Queen should not be played too early in the game; but here the Queen is not going too far afield and is not exposed to counterattack.

> **5.** ... ...   **P—Q 3**

Sooner or later, Black has to play this move to give his King Pawn really secure protection.

That security is obtained at the cost of two inconveniences. The diagonal (and hence the mobility) of Black's King Bishop, is cut down considerably by ... P—Q 3. Secondly, Black's Knight at Q B 3 is now "pinned." The Knight cannot move, for to do so would expose his King to attack. *Pinned pieces*, one readily realizes, *forfeit much of their mobility*.

> **6. P—B 3**   ... ...

Unlike Black, White is in a position to set up a formidable-looking Pawn center (Pawns at K 4 and Q 4). He ad-

vances the Queen Bishop Pawn to support the coming
P—Q 4.

6. ... ... **P—Q Kt 4**

The pin on Black's Queen Knight is annoying, so he
drives off the pinning Bishop in order to have more freedom of action.

7. B—Kt 3 **B—Kt 5**

Black decides to do a little pinning on his own.

Diagram 2

Black pins White's King Knight

Just as Black's Queen Knight was pinned after 5 ...
P—Q 3, White's King Knight is now pinned. (If the
Knight moves, White loses his Queen in return for only
a Bishop.)

But there is a difference between the two kinds of pins.
When Black's Knight was pinned, it would have been an
illegal move to move the Knight; for it is against the laws
of chess to expose one's King to attack. Here White's
Knight, though pinned, can move, without violating the
laws of chess. A Knight move would be legal, but nonsensi-

cal. The Queen is worth three times as much as a Bishop, hence moving the pinned Knight is unthinkable.

Once more we perceive how pinning *reduces the pinned piece's mobility*.

8.   P—Q R 4   ... ...

White wanted to play 8 P—Q 4, but he realized (see Diagram 2) that this would lose a Pawn for him, thus: 8 P—Q 4?, P × P; 9 P × P, Kt × Q P! Black's Knight move in the foregoing variation is based on the pin.

Thus, if 10 Kt × Kt, B × Q; and Black has won the Queen for only two minor pieces. (As the Queen is worth three minor pieces, the pin is operative and White cannot successfully play 8 P—Q 4).

After White's last move 8 P—Q R 4, Black must do something about the threat to his Queen Knight Pawn. This Pawn is attacked twice (by White's Queen and his Queen Rook Pawn) and defended only once (by Black's Queen Rook Pawn).

8.   ... ...   Kt—Q R 4

Black temporizes by counterattacking against White's unprotected Bishop at his Q Kt 3 square.

Straightforward defense by means of 8 ... Q R—Kt 1 was Black's best course. In that event, Black's Queen Knight Pawn would be adequately guarded: twice attacked, twice defended.

9.   B—B 2   ... ...

By safeguarding this Bishop, White renews the attack on Black's Queen Knight Pawn.

Now Black must do something about the attacked Pawn. But he doesn't!

Diagram 3

Black's Queen Knight Pawn is attacked

At this point it is not so easy to defend the Queen Knight Pawn. For example: 9 ... Q R—Kt 1; 10 P × P. Now Black makes the sad discovery that the natural-looking 10 ... P × P will not do because it allows White to win a piece by 11 R × Kt.

But (after 9 ... Q R—Kt 1; 10 P × P), the alternative 10 ... R × P is likewise unsatisfactory; for then comes 11 B—R 4, pinning the Rook and winning it for a Bishop.*

Black's best course is 9 ... B—Q 2. This renounces his aggressive pin, but it gives his menaced Pawn adequate protection.

9. ... ...   Kt—Kt 2?

Black completely misses the point, losing a Pawn outright.

---

* A Rook is worth, roughly, a Bishop (or Knight) and two Pawns. Hence it is materially advantageous to win a Rook for a Bishop (or Knight). This is called "winning the Exchange."

10. P × P   ... ...

Now Black has nothing better than 10 ... P × P; 11
Q × P ch, B—Q 2; 12 R × R, B × Q; 13 R × Q ch, K × R;
when White is a clear Pawn to the good.

10. ... ...   **Q—Kt 1?**

A new blunder, which should lose a second Pawn.

11. P—Q 4?   ... ...

But White is in turn blind to his opportunity. By simply
playing 11 P × P, White would win a second Pawn—one
passed and far advanced toward queening.

White's advance of the Queen Pawn is a good move in
itself. It is queried here only because White has overlooked the win of a second Pawn.

11. ... ...   **B × Kt**
12. P × B   **P—B 4?**

Again Black overlooks that he has a Pawn *en prise*
(subject to capture).

Relatively better is 12 ... P—Q R 4; avoiding further
material loss.

13. B—K 3?   ... ...

Black's lapse has again allowed White to win another
Pawn; but White misses his opportunity.

13. ... ...   **B P × P**

This capture and the following one are open to the
objection that *the Pawn exchanges create more scope for
White's Bishops.* Clear diagonals enormously enhance a

Bishop's power. Hence it is to Black's interest to keep the position closed as much as possible.

Such a policy is all the more essential in view of the fact that Black's development is seriously in arrears. With his remaining Bishop still at home, Black cannot castle for some time. This leaves his King in an insecure state, once more leading to the conclusion that *Black should avoid opening up the game.*

14.	B P × P	K P × P
15.	B × P	... ...

Diagram 4

Centralization and decentralization

It is interesting to compare the effectiveness of White's Bishop at Q 4 with that of Black's Queen.

The Bishop is centralized, powerfully posted on a key center square; and points in four different directions. (So we see that one of the useful aspects of having pieces in the center is that they can be poised for action on different fronts.)

Black's Queen, theoretically a much more powerful piece, is functioning at about ten per cent of its maximum strength. The Queen is *decentralized*. The same is true of Black's Knight on his Q N 2 square.

The ineffectual placement of Black's pieces explains why there is nothing faulty in White's failure to castle. Black's King is a potential victim of attack because Black's development is bad. White's King is in no danger because his development is good.

15.	... ...	**Kt—B 4?**	

Again Black overlooks that his Rook Pawn is under attack. This time White sees it.

16.	**P × P**	**Kt/B 3—Q 2**	

Black's game is now definitely beyond salvation.

17.	**Kt—B 3**	**Q × P?**	

A final blunder. Before making far-ranging captures with the Queen, one must weigh the consequences carefully. The significant factor here is the disquieting position of the Queen on the long diagonal, vulnerable to attack by White's centralized Bishop on Q 4.

Diagram 5

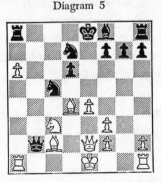

The vulnerable Queen

White can exploit the situation by playing 18 Kt—Kt 5!, attacking the Queen. Black's only counter worthy of notice is 18 ... Q—Kt 5 ch. But then 19 B—B 3 attacks the Queen, and leaves Black with nothing better than the loss of a piece (19 ... Kt—Q 6 ch) in order to make room for his Queen at his Q B 4 square.

This loss of material, coupled with Black's enormous positional inferiority, would leave him in a thoroughly hopeless state.

18.   Castles?   ... ...

Intent on protecting his attacked Rook, White overlooks his opportunity of winning a piece.

Now White threatens to win the Black Queen with 19 K R—Kt 1.

Black should meet this threat with 18 ... Q—Kt 1, with a lost game, but at least temporarily retaining his Queen!

Diagram 6*

Black overreaches himself

* One of the reasons for supplying Diagram 6 is to enable you to review the mechanics of castling. Compare the position of White's King and King Rook in Diagram 5 and Diagram 6.

18.   ... ...   R × P??

The idea behind this move is that if White tries 19 K R—Kt 1?? (hoping to win the Queen), Black replies 19 ... R × R! (pinning the remaining White Rook) and winning a whole Rook for Black.

Black also sees that if 19 R × R, N × R; 20 Q × Kt, Q × B; and Black is even in material. But Black has not calculated far enough ahead. There follows: 21 Q—B 8 ch!, K—K 2; 22 Kt—Q 5 ch, and White wins the Queen. But after 22 ... K—K 3; White does not bother with the Queen, because he is stalking higher game: 23 Q—K 8 ch, B—K 2; 24 Q × B mate!

This variation should be studied repeatedly until you have mastered its mechanics. The point is that Black has endangered his King by poor and dilatory development, and has increased his troubles by gallivanting after a distant Pawn. The result is that Black's miserable King, deserted by his forces, falls an easy prey to the attack of White's ideally placed troops.

19.   Kt—Kt 5!   Resigns

For after 19 ... Q—Kt 5 (forced); there follows 20 B— B 3. Black's Queen is trapped, and is lost for only a minor piece (Bishop or Knight).

SUMMARY: Black neglected his development, overlooked obvious captures, lost material, developed his pieces on poor squares. At the decisive moment, he exposed his King *and* Queen to decisive attack!

II

Guard Your King Adequately

INEXPERIENCED players who are bent on attacking at all cost, are often careless about the welfare of their own King. Such negligence is particularly risky when some avenue of hostile approach to the King is already available in a given position.

It ought to be obvious that we ought not to embark on offensive action if our own King is likely to be endangered by the withdrawal of protective forces. The risk ought to be doubly obvious when our development has not proceeded to a point at which we have sufficient strength for attack, as well as sufficient strength for the protection of our own King.

These things *ought* to be obvious, but generally they are not. Rough-and-ready players who have never studied the game may need years to learn fairly simple truths which may become immediately available from the study of *typical* games.

The following game, for example, is a sermon on the consequences of neglecting the safety of one's King. The moral is an unforgettable one.

King's Gambit

White	Black
1. P—K 4	P—K 4

The purpose behind these moves has been explained on page 14.

2. P—K B 4	... ...

In the first game, White attacked Black's King Pawn by developing his King Knight: 2 Kt—K B 3.

Here White attacks the King Pawn by advancing his own King Bishop Pawn. Quite a different picture. White obviously seeks the removal of Black's King Pawn from his K 4 square, permitting an eventual P—Q 4 by White. In that case, White will monopolize the important center squares. Black pieces will be unable to play to Black's Q B 4, Q 4, K 4 and K B 4 squares; for all these squares will be commanded by White's center Pawns.

White has another object in playing 2 P—K B 4: he wants to open the King Bishop file for attack against Black's K B 2 square, traditionally the most vulnerable square in openings of this character.

2.	B—B 4

An enormously interesting reply.

(See Diagram 7)

Black's Bishop move raises two fascinating problems: (1) is the Bishop move tactically feasible? and (2) what is the move supposed to accomplish?

The feasibility of 2 ... B—B 4 seems questionable on the ground that Black allows his King Pawn to be cap-

Diagram 7

Black offers a tainted Pawn

---

tured. But this permission is more deceptive than real. For after 3 P × P??, White is as good as lost. There follows 3. ... Q—R 5 ch!; 4. K—K 2, Q × K P mate! Or 3. ... Q—R 5 ch!; 4. P—K Kt 3, Q × K P ch, followed by 5 ... Q × R; with an enormous material advantage for Black, assuring him an easy win.

So we see that while we must be vigilant in considering all possible captures, we must also be vigilant in appraising the consequences of such captures. This is less of a chore than it sounds; in this case, for example, the faulty capture is immediately answered by a brutal refutation.

This answers the first question: 2. ... B—B 4 is tactically feasible. Now for our second question: what does 2. ... B—B 4 accomplish?

In the first place, it is a developing move, and a good one. (After the lifeless 2. ... P—Q 3, for example, Black's King Bishop would be hemmed in for good, thus reducing Black to a permanently restricted position.)

Also, 2. ... B—B 4 is a preparatory move for Black's castling. This is an important consideration for players who realize that castling automatically increases the King's security.

There is still another side to 2. ... B—B 4: it helps to restrain White's liberating and aggressive P—Q 4. Thus 2. ... B—B 4 is part of Black's fight for control of the center.

Finally, 2. ... B—B 4 has one more important facet. Being directed along the diagonal to White's K Kt 1 square, Black's Bishop makes it impossible for White to castle King-side even after his King Knight and King Bishop have moved. We will dwell on this later on in more detail.

3.   Kt—K B 3   ... ...

A good developing move. It prevents ... Q—R 5 ch and exerts additional pressure on the center, so that White can really menace the capture of the King Pawn.

At K B 3, the Knight is also ideally posted to support the advance of his Queen Pawn.

We are now beginning to see how much of the opening play is bound up with a struggle for advantage in the center.

3.   ... ...   P—Q 3

A nonchalant follow-up to his second move. Again the King Pawn seems inadequately guarded.

(See Diagram 8)

Careful examination shows that Black's King Pawn is adequately guarded; he relies on a finesse.

This is the point: after 4. P × P, P × P; 5. Kt × P, Black regains the Pawn by a double attack, either 5. ... Q—R 5 ch or 5. ... Q—Q 5. Note that 5. ... Q—Q 5 not

Diagram 8

Must Black lose a Pawn?

---

only attacks White's advanced Knight but also threatens
6 ... Q—B 7 mate. White's only parry is 6. Kt—Q 3 (meet-
ing both threats!), but then 6. ... Q × K P ch regains the
Pawn with the better game for Black.

So White forgets about the King Pawn for a while and
concentrates on his development—a sound decision.

4. B—B 4   Kt—Q B 3

Black likewise plays a good developing move, finally
giving his King Pawn overt protection.

Now White would like to castle, but he cannot do so.
Black's Bishop at Q B 4 commands the square (White's
K Kt 1) on which White's King would land. The laws of
chess forbid moving one's King into check; hence they
forbid castling into check.

(See Diagram 9)

What to do? How is White to solve the dilemma? He
hits on a resourceful solution:

5. P—B 3   ... ...

Diagram 9

White cannot castle

By advancing his Queen Bishop Pawn, he hopes to make P—Q 4 possible. In this way the Black Bishop's diagonal will be covered up, and White will be able to castle.

But there is still more to the text move: if White succeeds in playing P—Q 4, he will secure the monopoly in the center at which he has been aiming from the beginning of the game.

Black is in a quandary: he wants to scuttle White's plan, but he has no direct means of applying further pressure in the center. No direct means. But how about indirect means?

5.   ... ...   B—K Kt 5!

(See Diagram 10)

Again we see an example of pinning (as on page 17). Black pins the Knight, and thereby robs the pinned piece of any pressure on the center.

Concretely, this means that White must not play 6.

Diagram 10

Black pins the Knight

P—Q 4?, P × Q P; 7. P × P, Kt × P; 8. Kt × Kt??, B × Q;
and Black has a crushing, winning advantage. Of course, it
is unthinkable that White will fall into this catastrophe.
But here, precisely, we see the power of the pin. Its power
of restraint is so compelling that White's thoughts are
derailed from his objective.

6.   Q—Kt 3??   ... ...

But this is all wrong. White is so bothered by the pin
that he reacts instinctively by unpinning his Knight. And
the move he selects is certainly seductive: he threatens
B × P ch as well as Q × P. Yet, as we shall see, the Queen
move is disastrous.

Was there a better line? There was, and a little logical
reasoning suggests it at once. Let us recapitulate: White
wants to play P—Q 4, which would signify strategical
defeat for Black. The advance of the Pawn to Q 4 is prevented by the pinning Bishop. Therefore: drive away the
pinning Bishop!

The right move, then, is 6. P—K R 3!, attacking the

Bishop. If the Bishop retreats (say 6. ... B—Q 2), then
7. P—Q 4 is the move. Or if 6. ... B × Kt (best); 7 Q × B,
followed by P—Q 3 and B—K 3. In that case, White has
been prevented from playing P—Q 4, but he has a rea-
sonable development and will be able to castle into safety.

| 6. ... ... | B × Kt! |

Black ignores White's threats, perceiving that they lack
real sting.

Diagram 11

Who is attacking?!

Now White sees that 7. B × P ch is worthless. For example: 7. ... K—B 1; 8 P × B, Q—R 5 ch; 9. K—Q 1,
Kt—R 4; 10. Q—R 4, K × B; 11. Q × Kt, Q—B 7!; 12.
Q × B P ch, Kt—K 2. In that case, White's game is shat-
tered: his King is mortally menaced, he has no development, his Queen is far afield.

And here we see the flaw in 6. Q—Kt 3?? There is a
fatal breach in White's Pawn structure, and Black's Queen
invades with a decisive attack. White's "attack" is futile,
and his defense is crippled.

| 7. P × B | Q—R 5 ch |
| 8. K—Q 1 | ... ... |

The foregoing exchange has made it impossible for White to interpose a Pawn in reply to Black's Queen check.

| 8. | ... ... | Q—R 4 |
| 9. | Q × P | ... ... |

This hastens the end, despite White's formidable threats of Q × R ch or Q × Kt ch. When your King is in danger, such threats dwindle to nothing.

| 9. | ... ... | Q × B P ch |
| 10. | K—B 2 | ... ... |

On 10 K—K 1, Black forces checkmate with 10 ... B—B 7 ch; 11 K—B 1, B—Kt 6 disch; 12 K—Kt 1, Q—B 7 mate.

| 10. | ... ... | Q × K P ch |

If now 11 K—Kt 3, Black wins White's Queen by 11 ... Kt—R 4 ch. This is interesting: Black wins the White Queen by a Knight fork, and he also wins the Queen through discovered attack with his own Queen!

| 11. | P—Q 3 | ... ... |

Diagram 12

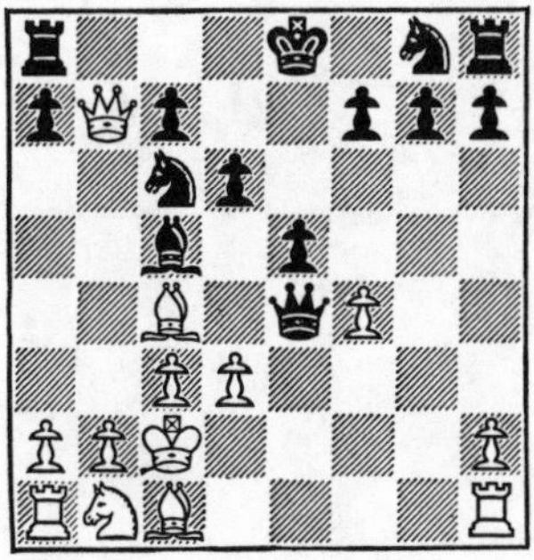

Black wins the Queen!

11. ... ...   Kt—Q 5 ch!

Resigns

After 12 P × Kt, Q × Q; White's situation is quite hope-less, in view of his crushing material loss.

SUMMARY: White fought consistently for control of the center, but then suddenly allowed himself to be distracted by a superficial chance for attack. The result was a fatal weakening of his King's position, leading to abrupt defeat.

III

Tame the Attack by Exchanging
Where Possible

PRACTICALLY every chessplayer prefers attack to defense. Attacking, we do as we please, and make the other fellow worry. What would be the fun of chess if we were always on the run, always trying to figure out what the opponent is up to, always trying to keep one step ahead of his threats? Too much like real life!

So runs the average player's thinking about chess. However, defense has its place in chess just as much as the attack. There is a solid thrill of satisfaction in defending resourcefully, skirting danger and living to tell the tale; a feeling of self-reliance is developed which provides one of the most pleasurable aspects of playing chess.

When you come to think of it, this reluctance to defend is a kind of spiritual laziness which we must all resist and overcome. Chess, like life, has its downs as well as ups. When we school ourselves to become hard-boiled defensive players, we are not only better chessplayers but better human beings as well.

And now for the specific lesson embodied in this game. One of the most effective defensive techniques is to exchange pieces wherever possible. This helps you to weather the attack because it reduces the number of enemy forces which are in a position to harm your King. Exchanging is all the more in order, when, as in the following game, the defender is ahead in material and can well afford to return some of the booty in exchange for a diminuendo of the fury of the attack.

Muzio Gambit

White	Black
1. P—K 4	P—K 4
2. P—K B 4	P × P

Here Black captures the gambit Pawn, bravely accepting the challenge implicit in White's second move. Regarding White's aims, see page 26.

| 3. Kt—K B 3 | P—K Kt 4 |

Modern theory views this move with a very jaundiced eye. Why neglect your development and rip up your King-side Pawn formation for the sake of retaining a mere Pawn?

Modern usage favors 3 ... P—Q 4 or 3 ... Kt—K B 3. By playing these moves, Black promotes his development and fights for the center. This leads to a type of game in which Black can strive for the initiative, instead of allowing himself to be relegated to a risky defensive task.

| 4. B—B 4 | P—Kt 5 |
| 5. Castles!? | ... ... |

Diagram 13

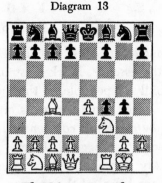

The Muzio sacrifice

Having offered a Pawn, White now offers a piece. This daring sacrifice, which leads to a wealth of slashing attacks, goes back at least as far as the days of Renaissance Italy, but became really popular only toward the end of the eighteenth century. In accepting the sacrifice, Black is foolhardy indeed if he does not envision a speedy return of some of the sacrificed material in order to safeguard his King.

5.   ... ...   P × Kt

Black has made nothing but Pawn moves. His lack of development invites aggression!

6.   B × P ch!?   ... ...

And this second, rather uncommon, sacrifice is generally termed "the wild Muzio."

That nickname is a warning. The second sacrifice is so brutal, so surprising, that it is likely to leave Black in a befuddled state of mind. He may be so dazed that he will find himself with a lost game before he is quite aware of what is going on.

6.	... ...	K × B
7.	Q × P	Q—B 3

Black's lonesome King needs company. For both players, *time* is now of the essence. Black must strive to develop his pieces as rapidly as possible, so that he can shield his King efficiently. White must bring *his* attack to bear on the hostile King *before Black can consolidate his position.*

With two pieces to the good, Black's chief defensive weapon is already apparent. When opportunity offers, he can return a good deal of the extra material—perhaps give up his Queen for a Rook—and in this way paralyze the attack. In giving up the material, however, Black must part with it in return for White units which *participate in the attack.*

8.	P—K 5!?	... ...

Line-opening must be the clue to White's play.

8.	... ...	Q × P

Diagram 14

Strike while the iron is hot!

9.	P—B 3?	... ...

Strangely tame. White must not lose any time. Hence
9 P—Q 4! was the move. Then if 9 ... Q × P ch; 10 B—K
3! (taking advantage of the fact that Black's King Bishop
Pawn is pinned, so that if 10 ... Q × B ch?; 11 Q × Q,
and Black cannot recapture because his King Bishop
Pawn is pinned.)

In the parenthetical variation, by the way, Black profits
little from having three minor pieces for the Queen. Ordinarily this would signify a material advantage for Black;
but here White's Queen and King Rook are available for
the attack, so that Black's surrender of material serves
no useful purpose.

9.	P—Q 3

More to the point now is 9 ... B—R 3!; developing, and
also guarding the vital King Bishop Pawn, whose prolonged life keeps the dangerous King Bishop file closed.

10. P—Q 4	Q—K B 4
11. B × P	... ...

Compare the previous note. White now has the King
Bishop file completely open—the prime objective of the
King's Gambit. Black is by no means lost, but his defensive task has become much more tortuous with the opening of the crucial file.

11.	Kt—Q B 3

Beginning to mobilize the Queen-side pieces—a good
idea, as will be seen.

12. Q—K2	... ...

Diagram 15

White threatens to . . . threaten

White threatens to move his Bishop (say 13 B—Kt 3), pinning, and winning, Black's Queen. But this threat is only a "threat."

Black can simply play 12 ... Kt—B 3!, developing, and shielding his King. Then, in the event of 13 B—Kt 3, he beats off the attack by simplifying: 13 ... Q × R ch; 14 Q × Q, B—K 3; 15 B—R 4, B—Kt 2. With a Rook, Bishop and Knight for Queen and Pawn, Black is ahead in material, and White's attack is pretty well spent with the disappearance of his valuable King Rook from the King Bishop file.

12. ... ...   **K—Kt 3**

Black is overcautious, and actually courts danger for that very reason!

13. B—Kt 3   **... ... ...**

(*See Diagram 16*)

Black is lucky. He missed the bus, but he can still catch the next one! By playing 13 ... Q × R ch!, followed by 14

Diagram 16

Black still has an adequate defense

... Kt—B 3; he is still quite safe: the attack is beaten off, and his material advantage will decide the game in his favor.

13.   ... ...   Q—K Kt 4?

Again Black fails to make the most of his chances.

It is worth while here to make an important point, namely that the general run of players are very reluctant to give up the Queen, even for more than adequate compensation. This unwillingness is partly due to great respect for the powers of the Queen, and partly to the fact that only the most experienced players are adept at coordinating the powers of minor pieces and Rooks against the Queen.

It it therefore useful to take positions such as the one in Diagram 16, and experiment with the task of proving the superiority of Rook and two minor pieces against the Queen.

14.   Q—K 8 ch   Resigns (!)

Even Black's resignation is a minor blunder! After 14 ... K—R 3; 15 B—B 4, Q × B; 16 R × Q, B—K 2; Black will lose because of the exposed position of his King; but the win still remains to be demonstrated.

Likewise, after 14 ... K—R 3; 15 Q × B ch, Q—Kt 2; 16 B—B 4 ch, K—Kt 3; 17 Q—K 8 ch, Q—B 2; 18 Q × Q ch, K × Q; 19 B—K 5 dis ch, Kt—B 3!; Black can put up quite a fight, as he is only a Pawn down in the endgame.

Granted, these variations are not easy for the average player to calculate. But why give White credit for seeing them, and resign so quickly and spinelessly? This premature resignation is only the final example of Black's collapse under pressure.

SUMMARY: Black was unaware of his resources for defense. He did not appreciate the value of exchanging as a means of taking the sting out of his opponent's attack. The shock of being under attack was too much for him.

IV

Avoid Indiscriminate Pawn-Grabbing

Is THERE a contradiction between this advice and the theme of the first game? No; a player must be vigilant in looking out for every possible kind of capture, but that does not mean that he must grab everything that is not nailed down.

It is unfortunate, but true, that players tend to one extreme or the other. In fact, the same player may be guilty of both faults! Strictly speaking, only one fault is involved here: overlooking a bona fide capture bespeaks the same kind of feckless negligence as making an impulsive capture which leads straight to perdition.

And the cure? The first step on the way to improvement is to be aware of the flaw in one's play. Many a player continues to make the same kind of mistake for ten, twenty, thirty years without perceiving that the individual mistakes group themselves into a small number of distinct categories. That is to say, of a thousand specific mistakes, three hundred may be of a certain kind, another three hundred may belong to another category, the remaining four hundred to still another group.

The *number* of mistakes we may make is endless; the *kinds* of mistakes we may make are strictly limited as to type and character. And so, learning *one* principle may help you to avoid hundreds, perhaps thousands, of mistakes!

PETROFF DEFENSE

White	Black
1. P—K 4	P—K 4
2. Kt—K B 3	Kt—K B 3

In the first game (page 14) Black defended his attacked King Pawn with the developing move 2 ... Kt—Q B 3.

Here Black also responds with a developing move, but it is counterattacking rather than defensive in nature. And this inspires us with a feeling of distrust: is Black justified in counterattacking so early in the game?

Without wanting to give a definite opinion at this point, let us say this: the skeptical attitude is justified. Black's bid for counterplay must be managed judiciously. If he proceeds in an oversanguine mood, he can easily put his resources under an intolerable strain.

3. Kt × P	... ...

White takes; a perfectly safe procedure. *But it is not safe to capture in reply!*

(*See Diagram 17*)

Now Black's proper course is 3 ... P—Q 3; 4 Kt—K B 3, Kt × P. Then if White pins the Knight with 5 Q—K 2, Black defends easily and safely with 5 ... Q—K 2.

3.	Kt × P?

A typical mistake (thoughtless recapture) which has

Diagram 17

Handle with care!

---

been repeated for generations. Black fails to realize that the complete opening of the King file may bring dangers with it because of a possible pin. His advanced Knight is now exposed to a dangerous attack.

4.   Q—K 2!   ... ...

White, on the other hand, is fully alive to the potentialities of this position. If Black's menaced Knight retreats, there follows 5 Kt—B 6 dis ch, winning Black's Queen!

Thus we see that Black's slovenly third move has a price tag on it. He will not be able to extricate himself without loss of some kind.

For example, if he defends the attacked Knight with 4 ... P—Q 4 or 4 ... P—K B 4; there follows 5 P—Q 3, and the wretched Knight is unable to retreat because of the crushing reply 6 Kt—B 6 dis ch.

4.   ... ...   **Q—K 2**

Realizing that he cannot save his Knight by direct methods, Black decides to rely on a counterpin.

Diagram 18

Black's counterattack will be refuted

5. Q × Kt   P—Q 3

This will regain the piece, as White's attacked Knight is pinned and cannot retreat. But White will remain at least a Pawn to the good.

6. P—Q 4   P—K B 3

Black wants to regain the piece without losing a Pawn.

7. P—K B 4   ... ...

And White is equally stubborn about winning the Pawn!

7. ... ...   Kt—Q 2

He is still intent on avoiding the loss of a Pawn.

8. Kt—Q B 3!   ... ...

White's superior development and the initiative which derives from it, enable him to get rid of the pin advantageously. The great merit of his last move is that it guards the Queen (and therefore threatens, at last, to withdraw the pinned Knight); at the same time, White's last move embodies the aggressive possibility of Kt—Q 5.

Once more we see that inadequate development helps to defeat the execution of a tactical idea (in this case, Black's pin). Contrariwise, superior development helps to assure the success of a tactical idea (White's resistance to the pin).

Diagram 19

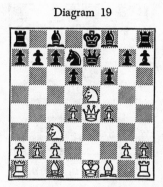

White attacks and defends

8.	Q P × Kt

As has been explained, the Knight must be captured now or never.

9. Kt—Q 5	... ...

An embarrassing move for Black: if he plays 9 ... Q—K 3??; 10 Kt × Q B P ch forks Black's King and Queen.

And if 9 ... Q—Q 1 (certainly the lesser evil); White comes out a valuable Pawn to the good after 10 B P × P, P × P; 11 P × P, etc.

9.	Q—Q 3?

Black succumbs to the will-o'-the-wisp of still trying to save the Pawn! This is an impossible task, for Black's

Queen cannot try to save the Pawn and at the same time guard against the terrible forking threat of Kt × P ch.

| 10. | B P × P | P × P |
| 11. | P × P | ... ... |

Diagram 20

The power of the pin!

Now Black finds that there are more pins than he can contend with:

If 11 ... Q × P; 12 Kt × P ch forks his King and his Queen Rook because his pinned Queen cannot capture the forking Knight. (Or, more simply: 11 ... Q × P; 12 Q × Q ch, Kt × Q; 13 Kt × P ch with the same result.)

And if 11 ... Kt × P; 12 B—K B 4, with a pin that wins Black's Knight!

| 11. | ... ... | Q—Q B 3 |

The only move left to guard the Queen Bishop Pawn, but it proves inadequate.

| 12. | B—Q Kt 5! | ... ... |

Neat play. If 12 ... Q × B; 13 Kt × P ch, forking Black's King and Queen.

| 12. | ... ... | Q—B 4 |

The only move left to Black if he is to continue defending the Queen Bishop Pawn against the forking threat.

| 13. | B—K 3! | Resigns |

No matter how Black plays, he must lose the Queen. This game is an effective example of the drawbacks to an early development of the Queen. White was able to develop his Queen with impunity because he was punishing an earlier transgression by Black.

SUMMARY: Black's thoughtless capture on the third move ruined his game. In making captures or recaptures, you must be on the lookout for any tactical devices (pins, forks, etc.) on your opponent's part which will stamp your move as a blunder. The punishment will be particularly drastic if your development is inferior to that of your opponent.

V

Train Your Attack on Black's
Vulnerable K B 2 Square

ONE of the most characteristic features of games between
inexperienced players is that one or both Kings are likely
to be exposed to crushing attack.

There are many reasons for this. One is that such
players are likely to embark on any project, useless or
useful, which happens to appeal to them; unless they
have made a serious study of the game, they are unaware
of the basic need for quick development of their pieces
and for early castling to safeguard the King. And quick
development is a fundamental requirement: without it,
you cannot castle early; or, having castled, you will lack
the disposable forces with which to defend your belea-
guered King.

Another reason why the King is often subjected to dis-
tressing and even fatal dangers, is simply that the average player is not familiar with the standard methods and
techniques for smoking out a vulnerable King.

In openings, for example, which begin 1 P—K 4, P—K

4; the vulnerable point, above all, is the square K B 2 in both camps. Is it not significant that our two most venerable traps* are both based on the vulnerable state of the K B 2 square?

Again, some of the oldest openings and attacks (the Giuoco Piano, the King's Gambits, the Fegatello or "Fried Liver" Attack), dating back at least three centuries, bear witness to the lasting virulence of this theme: attack on the K B 2 square. When the great Italian chess analysts of the late-Renaissance period began their pioneering study of opening theory, the theme of attack against Black's K B 2 square was the most obvious and, to them, the most impressive of all possible attacking techniques.

Later on, as great masters began to appear on the scene, as better books were written, as chess periodicals made their appearance and brilliant international tournaments and individual matches became regular institutions, chess theory proliferated enormously; technique became ever more refined, themes more numerous and more subtle.

So it is with the individual chessplayer. He passes through the same development in his own life-history as the chess world has experienced as a collective group. In due course, he will be adept in the Indian Defenses, be familiar with the latest finesses in the Catalan System and the minority Pawn attack in the Exchange Variation of the Queen's Gambit Declined. But, if he is the typical reader for whom this book is intended, such esoteric matters are at present beyond his ken, and he will find it more useful to study the pros and cons of the attack against the K B 2 square. For to learn how to manage

---

* The Fool's Mate: 1 P—K B 3?, P—K 4; 2 P—K Kt 4??, Q—R 5 mate. The Scholar's Mate: 1 P—K 4, P—K 4; 2 B—B 4, B—B 4; 3 Q—R 5, Kt—Q B 3??; 4 Q × B P mate.

that attack, and how to defend against it, is one of the most important phases of every chessplayer's development.

RUY LOPEZ

	White	Black
1.	P—K 4	P—K 4
2.	Kt—K B 3	Kt—Q B 3
3.	B—Kt 5	P—Q R 3

As we know from the first game (page 15), Black can safely venture this move without having to fear the loss of a Pawn; for if 4 B × Kt, Q P × B; 5 Kt × P, Q—Q 5 (or 5 ... Q—Kt 4); and Black regains the Pawn.

4.	B—R 4	P—Q Kt 4

Here Black's timing is careless. The right course is 4 ... Kt—B 3 (developing a piece!) followed by 5 ... B—K 2 (developing another piece!) and 6 ... Castles (safeguarding the King!).

The Pawn move, on the other hand, does not contribute to Black's development and has the flaw of driving White's King Bishop to a menacing diagonal.

5.	B—Kt 3	Kt—B 3

The questionable order of moves adopted by Black leaves him a move short of being able to castle. This gives White his opportunity to create trouble:

(*See Diagram 21*)

6.	Kt—Kt 5	... ...

There is a sound objection to moving a piece more than once in the opening, unless some very good reason

Diagram 21

Black's K B 2 square is vulnerable!

---

can be offered for the extra moves. In this case, the double attack on Black's King Bishop Pawn can be considered "good reason"!

If Black had played as recommended in the note to his fourth move, he would now be perfectly safe. As matters stand, however, Black's next move is the only one he has to break the force of the double attack against his vulnerable K B 2 square.

| 6. | ... ... | P—Q 4 |
| 7. | P × P | ... ... |

And now Black's wisest course is not to recapture the Pawn, but to play 7 ... Kt—Q 5, removing White's ominous Bishop. But Black does not appreciate the dangerous character of this position.

| 7. | ... ... | Kt × P |

It may be that the most expert, searching analysis can establish that this move is perfectly sound. Be that as it may, no player should voluntarily expose himself to the risks and privations which result from the text move!

8.   Kt × B P!   ... ...

Diagram 22

The bombshell bursts on K B 2!

White's last move is on the order of the sacrifice in the famous "Fried Liver" Attack. Black can hardly avoid capturing the Knight, after which his King will be exposed to a lasting attack and driven out to the middle of the board.

This explains why, in the note to White's 7th move, the peaceful alternative 7 ... Kt—Q 5 was recommended.

8.   ... ...   **K × Kt**
9.   Q—B 3 ch   ... ...

The plot thickens. The Queen check attacks Black's Knight on Q 4 for the second time, so that Black's only move worth considering is 9 ... K—K 3. But in that case the Black King is bound to find himself in the withering crossfire of White's pieces.

Black's worst difficulty is putting up with the fierce pinning pressure exerted by White's Bishop from his Q

Kt 3 square. And it was Black who drove the Bishop to that square!

    9. ... ...   **K—K 3**

Forced, as we have seen.

    10. **Kt—B 3**   ... ...

Good. He *intensifies the pin* on Black's miserable Knight, and now threatens 11 B × Kt ch, blowing Black's position to smithereens.

Diagram 23

Black's King is in mortal danger

    10. ... ...   **Kt/B 3—K 2**

Black gives the pinned Knight the needed protection, and begins to feel a little more secure, as he can support the Knight additionally with ... P—B 3 and/or ... B—Kt 2.

    11. **P—Q 4!**   ... ...

Quite right. Black must not be given time to consolidate his position, nor must he be allowed to recover from the shock of being made the target of such an unexpected sacrifice.

As we saw in the third game (page 35), there is a definite feeling of shock, of terror, in response to a brutal sacrifice at the K B 2 square. The crippling feeling of unpleasant surprise is reinforced by the intimacy of the blow; for a smash at the K B 2 square is like a dagger directed at the very heart of the hostile position.

| 11.   ... ... | P—B 3 |

Black hastens to give the pinned Knight more support. If, instead, 11 ... P × P?; 12 Q—K 4 ch is decisive, as Black loses a piece—and may lose his Queen Rook as well. For example: 11 ... P × P?; 12 Q—K 4 ch, K—B 2; 13 Kt × Kt, Kt × Kt; 14 B × Kt ch, followed by 15 B × R.

| 12.   B—Kt 5 | ... ... |

More pinning—now both Black Knights are pinned. One readily sees the paralyzing influence of these pins. They reduce the effectiveness of Black's forces to a point where White's minus in material is more theoretical than actual.

| 12.   ... ... | Q—Q 3 |

Black unpins one of the Knights at least. But, as Black's Queen will be subject to attack at her new square, it seems wiser to play ... B—Kt 2 at this stage.

| 13.   Castles Q R! | ... ... |

Castling on the Queen-side, in this case, is much stronger than castling on the other wing. White brings his Queen Rook to the Queen file at once, thereby enabling the Rook to participate in the pressure against Black's pinned Knight.

Diagram 24

White's Queen Rook strengthens the attack

Note that every move White has made since the sacrifice has contributed in some way to the progress of his attack. As for his opponent, the picture is grim: his King in the center, his pieces badly developed or not at all.

| 13. | ... ... | P—R 3 |

An expression of Black's discomfort: he wants to drive off one of the annoying Bishops. However, his game is beyond salvation.

14.	Kt—K 4	Q—B 2
15.	Kt—B 5 ch	K—Q 3
16.	P × P ch!!	... ...

(*See Diagram 25*)

White's attack is in full swing. One piece sacrificed, another one under attack, still another one sacrificed! Such play is very brilliant—true. But what is more significant is that the exposed position of Black's King allows White to take many liberties.

Black has only a choice of evils. If now, for example,

Diagram 25

More sacrifices!

---

16. ... K × P; 17. K R—K 1 ch, K—Q 3; 18. B/Kt 5 × Kt ch is crushing. On 18. ... B × B; there follows 19. R × Kt ch, P × R; 20. Q × P mate.

There are other ways to win, as well. The exposed position of Black's King is our surety that there are many roads to Rome (checkmate) in this case.

16.	... ...	K × Kt
17.	B—K 3 ch	... ...

And now if 17 ... Kt × B; 18 Q × Kt ch, K—Kt 5; 19 Q—Q B 3 mate.

With Black's King so far out on a limb, we are now in the realm of spectacular checkmates. White is two pieces down, but this simply does not signify in the face of the mortal King-hunt that is now in progress.

17.	... ...	K—Kt 5
18.	B × Kt	... ...

This Bishop has rendered yeoman service, but now White needs to clear the terrain for decisive mating action against Black's hounded, harried and isolated King.

| 18. ... ... | **Kt × B** |

The alternative 18 ... P × B allows the same kind of finish.

| **19. B—Kt 6!!** | ... ... |

Already two pieces down, White sacrifices a third for a forced mate. Again it must be emphasized that the extraordinary position of Black's King sanctions all manner of extraordinary measures against the helpless King.

Diagram 26

An elegant clearance sacrifice!

19.	... ...	**Q × B**
20.	Q—Q R 3 ch	K—B 5
21.	P—Kt 3 ch	K—B 6
22.	R—Q 3 mate!	

A striking finish. Black's King wandered from K 1 to K B 2 to K 3 to Q 3 to Q B 4 to Q Kt 5 to Q B 5 to Q B 6 and was then finally checkmated.

SUMMARY: This game emphasizes the vulnerability of the K B 2 square. As a rule, it is Black who is the victim, White having the first move and the more likely prospects

of a quick initiative. As we have seen, the sacrifice on
Black's K B 2 square has enormous "shock" value. Add
to this the sheer impossibility of the King's surviving
unscathed after running the gauntlet from K 1 to Q B 6,
and we are thoroughly convinced of the value of concen-
trating on the K B 2 square. This applies, of course, only
to openings in which the King Bishop is at Q B 4 or at
Q Kt 3—on the diagonal which strikes down at Black's
K B 2 square. Above all, the moral to be derived from
this game is: safeguard your King by early castling!

VI

Try to Force Open Files

AGAIN and again we emphasize the importance of development. It is a favorite theme of all chess teaching and all chess books. Assuming that you are now impressed with the importance of developing your pieces rapidly, we can proceed to a more advanced, but just as important, problem.

How do the pieces function once they are developed? How can we be certain that they will operate efficiently?

Once the pieces are developed, they need open lines: open files for the Rooks, long diagonals for the Bishops. Thus, in Diagram 24, White's Rook at Q 1 is doing nothing at the moment: its action is blocked by the White Pawn at his Q 4 square. But in Diagram 25, the impeding Pawn has captured on White's K 5 square; the Queen file is opened; the Queen Rook is active, and adds its vigorous assistance to the onslaught.

The same line of reasoning applies to the Bishops. Consider the situation in Diagram 2. The Black Bishop at his K Kt 5 square has a clear diagonal and plays a useful role pinning White's Knight. But the other Black Bishop (at his K B 1 square) has no scope to speak of. Its natural diagonal is blocked by the Pawn at Black's Q 3 square.

How about the White Bishops? (We are still studying Diagram 2.) White's Bishop at his Q Kt 3 square has a fine open diagonal and is effectively posted. His other Bishop (at his Q B 1 square) is momentarily blocked by his Queen Pawn, and thus has no mobility whatsoever. But once the Queen advances, the Bishop's diagonal will be opened; it will become an effectively developed piece. (In fact, as the game goes, it is this very Bishop that traps Black's Queen!)

So you see that if pieces are to function effectively, they must have scope for movement; the more scope, the better. This scope they obtain from open lines; the longer these lines, the better.

How do lines get opened? The most frequent cause of line-opening is a Pawn capture—a capture of a Pawn or by a Pawn. Returning to Diagram 25 again, we observe that in the ensuing play, the Queen file is opened for White when he plays 16 P × P ch. Go through any number of games, study the effect of captures made by Pawns. Repeatedly you will see that captures made by Pawns result in open lines.

So here you have acquired a valuable bit of information. You make Pawn captures and Pawn recaptures in order to win material or maintain material equality. Yet each such capture opens a line, and it enhances your planning skill considerably to be aware of this line-opening and *foresee how you can make use of it.*

GIUOCO PIANO

White	Black
1. P—K 4	P—K 4
2. Kt—K B 3	Kt—Q B 3

White attacks the King Pawn and Black defends, as in the first game (page 14).

3. B—B 4   ... ...

Whereas in the first game White played 3 B—Kt 5 (Ruy Lopez), he tries a different Bishop development here. The Bishop bears down at Black's K B 2 square.

3. ... ...   B—B 4

Black follows suit. The Italian name of this opening means "quiet game"—a suitable description for many of the rather placid lines which are a feature of this opening. However, the game may often take a lively turn later on.

4. P—Q 3   ... ...

White opens the diagonal for his Queen Bishop.

4. ... ...   Kt—B 3

Black replies with a good developing move.

Now 5 Kt—Kt 5 is utterly futile, as Black safeguards his King comfortably with the simple reply 5 ... Castles.

5. Castles   P—Q 3

Diagram 27

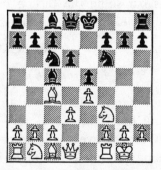

How should White continue his development?

The development of White's Queen Bishop is in order, and the best choice seems to be 6 B—K 3. Here the Bishop participates in the struggle for control of the center squares. (It is, as we shall see, important for White to keep his Q 4 square under his direct control.) After 6 B—K 3, B × B; 7 P × B, White obtains an open King Bishop file. This is an example of the manner in which Pawn captures result in open files.

6.   B—K Kt 5   ... ...

Not quite so good as 6 B—K 3. True, the text move is aggressive (it pins Black's King Knight); but it does not have the same effect that B—K 3 has in struggling for control of the center.

6.   ... ...   P—K R 3
7.   B—R 4?   ... ...

With this error of judgment, White burns his bridges behind him. Correct is 7 B—K 3, whereby White rectifies his previous error of judgment by bringing the Bishop back to the center.

In retreating the Bishop to K R 4, White does not realize that he is banishing the Bishop from the center, and thus greatly diminishing the usefulness of this piece.

7.   ... ...   B—K Kt 5

(See Diagram 28)

Black's pin on White's Knight promises to be troublesome. At this point Black threatens ... Kt—Q 5, reinforcing the pin. If White is eventually forced to recapture on his K B 3 square with his King Knight Pawn, a breach will be created in his castled position. His King will be

Diagram 28

Black's pin may be troublesome

exposed to attack, and his K R 3 square will no longer be guarded by the King Knight Pawn.

    8. P—B 3   ... ...

Good. White staves off these disagreeable possibilities by preventing ... Kt—Q 5. Expressed in technical language, the advance P—B 3 gives White a more powerful hold on the center than he had before advancing this Pawn.

    8. ... ...   **P—K Kt 4!**

The full strength of this fine move can best be appreciated as we proceed with the game and study its consequences.

    9. B—K Kt 3   ... ...

This much is already clear. White's Queen Bishop is sadly hemmed in and left with virtually no mobility. This underlines the error committed by White at his 7th move.

    9. ... ...   **P—K R 4!**

The immediate threat is ... P—R 5; winning a piece, as the unfortunate Bishop would be trapped.

White can of course save his Bishop, but only at the cost of making a weakening Pawn move.

10. P—K R 3   ... ...

Diagram 29

White's castled position is weakened

Why has White's castled position been weakened by the advance of the King Rook Pawn? The principle involved is a very important one.

Black has not yet castled. (The delay involves no danger in this case, as Black has an excellent development, while White has no possibilities of attack.) Not having castled, Black can freely advance his King-side Pawns without having to worry that this advance will weaken his King's position.

We have seen that Pawn captures result in open files. Black would be delighted to open the King Rook file, or the King Knight file, *and thus obtain an open file along which he could mount an attack against White's castled King.* However, to force Pawn exchanges when the White

Pawns are still on the second rank, is virtually impossible. Let one of the White Pawns in front of the King advance to the third or fourth rank, and forcing an exchange becomes rather easy.

To recapitulate: by retreating his Bishop to K R 4 instead of to K 3, White placed his Bishop in a situation where it was bound to be vulnerable to the advance of the hostile King-side Pawns. These Pawns have now advanced to a point where White must counter with a move of his King Rook Pawn to save the Bishop. This move (10 P—K R 3) will result in the opening of a file to be used against White's King.

10.	P—R 5!

So that if 11 P × B, P × B; with a wide-open King Rook file and the ideal attacking position which Black seeks.

11. B—R 2	... ...

White retreats, but the opening of a file is now inevitable.

11.	B—R 4

For now the coming ... P—Kt 5 will force open a file no matter how White plays.

12. Q—Kt 3	... ...

As in the second game (page 31), White runs away from the burdensome pin.

12.	P—Kt 5!

Diagram 30

Black forces the opening of a file

Now White is powerless against the opening of a file, either by his playing P × P or by Black's playing ... P × P.

13. Kt—Kt 5   ... ...

Interestingly enough, White has set up a counteraction of sorts against Black's K B 2 square. Thus, if Black plays 13 ... P—Kt 6 (apparently winning a piece because White's King Bishop Pawn is pinned—thus White's K B 2 square is also vulnerable!), White plays 14 B × P ch. This must not be answered by 14 ... B × B?? because of 15 Q × B mate. Nor can Black play 14 ... K—B 1 because of 15 Kt—K 6 ch forking Black's King and Queen. And after 14 ... K—K 2; 15 B × B keeps the game complicated.

13. ... ...   **Q—Q 2!**

Well played. Black guards his K B 2 square and retains all his positional trumps.

14. P × P   **Kt × Kt P**

Now Black has his open King Knight file, with all the

Diagram 32

Decision on the open file

One of Black's most serious threats is now 19 ... B × P!;
20 Kt × B, Q—Kt 6 ch; 21 K—R 1, B—B 6! This menaces
the sequel 22 ... B × P ch; 23 R × B, Q × R mate. Nor
can White play 22 P × B, Q × R mate. The splendid
harmony between Black's Rooks and Bishops produces
many pretty pinning motifs.

White can try (in the position of Diagram 32) 19 B ×
P, which looks plausible because it threatens to win
Black's Queen by 20 B—K 6 ch. But Black answers 19
B × P convincingly with 19 ... B × B; 20 Q × B, Q R—
K B 1. (Note that the capture of Black's King Bishop
Pawn has opened that file for Black!) Then, after 21 Q—
Kt 3, B × P; 22 Kt × B, R × Kt; Black's Queen and Rooks
all converge on White's K Kt 2 square for a quick mate.

These variations should be studied not only from the
point of view of mastering their tactical and technical
details, but also with an appreciation of the over-all con-
ception: murderous pressure along the open file against
an isolated King.

19.   Q—B 2   ... ...

Offering at least a modicum of help to his King. The Queen move gives his King Bishop Pawn much-needed protection.

19.	...	...	...	R—Kt 2

As logical as it is obvious. Black strengthens his grip on the open file by *doubling* his Rooks on it. This is a characteristic maneuver in similar positions, and enormously enhances Black's fire-power on the open file.

20.	Kt—R 3		...	... ...

A Knight is always poorly placed at the side of the board, as it has very few squares at its disposal. (The other Knight, at White's K R 3 square, has no moves at all!) However, White's chief interest right now is to get his Queen Rook into his defensive formation.

20.	...	...	...	Q R—Kt 1

Black has now attained his position of maximum power on the open file. An explosion is indicated!

21.	Q R—K B 1		...	... ...

White does the best he can—which happens not to be good enough.

(*See Diagram 33*)

21.	...	...	...	Q × P ch!

A Queen sacrifice is always enchanting; but a Queen sacrifice that evolves logically from first-class play is the most attractive of all.

22.	R × Q		R × R ch
23.	K—R 1		B—B 6

Diagram 33

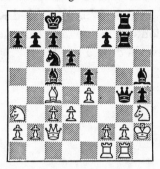

Black has a brilliant sacrifice

Black is still ruthlessly exploiting the open King Knight file. His threat is now 24 ... R × P mate. Such is the stark power of well-placed pieces on open lines!

24. Kt—K Kt 1 ... ...

Despite his material advantage, White cannot meet the threat successfully.

24. ... ... R × Kt dbl ch
25. K—R 2 R × R
Resigns

Black threatens 26 ... R—R 8 mate. White's only resource is to play 27 Q—Kt 1, when Black can simply play 27 ... R × Q; remaining a Rook and Bishop ahead. Or Black can play 27 ... R × P ch; 28 K—R 3, B—Kt 7 ch; leading to a quick mate.

SUMMARY: Black's play is a perfect model for the method of forcing open lines and exploiting them. Almost from the very beginning, Black realized that White's faulty retreat of his Queen Bishop could be utilized to force open a file against White's castled King. Thereafter, Black's application of the advantage of the open file could not have been excelled by a master.

VII

Watch for the Crisis

THE great Emanuel Lasker was once asked his opinion of one of his most famous rivals, David Janowski. This master was equipped with more than the average share of ingenuity, determination, courage, technical facility. Yet he never quite achieved the place to which his abilities seemed to entitle him.

"Janowski? Oh, he liked to/get favorable positions, and he knew how. But, once he had a good game, even a winning game, he would fiddle around with it endlessly, so that the win would fizzle out in a draw—and sometimes he would even lose! It almost seemed as if he didn't want to win. Poor Janowski!"

There are many players like that. They seem to be unaware that every game has its crisis—that one culminating point when the fate of the game is decided once for all. All the careful preparation, all the excellent *previous* play, go for nothing unless the fateful position is appraised correctly and handled energetically.

As we saw in the third game (page 35), this crucial problem may often arise in the case of defensive play.

One onslaught after another may be beaten off, until the attacker has one last chance. If his last desperate attack is repulsed, the attack is over, crushed; and he can resign. The defender, weary, excited, nervous from the continual strain of being harried, may be too tired to care by this time; or he may see the full significance of the situation, and may be overwhelmed by this last, great responsibility. Or, if he is a player with real grit and determination, he may rise to the occasion and beat back the attack.

What makes this problem rather obscure to most people is that chess is not a *physical* contest. The fact that all the fighting is on the mental level may disguise for many of us the fact that it *is* a contest. The easygoing player who takes the attitude that "chess is only a game" will never be the equal of the player who realizes that chess is more than a game; it is a clash of personalities, of opposing wills, of two egos that are figuratively clawing each other for victory.

Chess, of course, should not be taken too seriously. The relaxing feature of chess arises precisely from the fact that the outcome of a game, for most people, is of no world-shaking importance. Nevertheless, if we want to succeed in a game, we must apply to it the same determination, the same accurate appraisal, the same concentration that we try to apply to far more important matters. The relaxation arises from the fact that the outcome of the game is much less important than the outcome of an analogous struggle in "real life."

SICILIAN DEFENSE

White	Black
1. P—K 4	P—Q B 4

Black's first move is a departure from the previous openings we have seen. Black dispenses with the customary ... P—K 4 because he wishes to have an opening of his own choosing, free from any favorite or prepared variations that White may have had in mind.

2.	Kt—K B 3	Kt—Q B 3

As always, these Knight moves are excellent from the standpoint of development.

3.	P—Q 4	... ...

This early advance is the best procedure against the Sicilian. White opens up the position and greatly increases the scope of his pieces.

3.	... ...	P × P

The capture is Black's best course. On other moves, White can play P—Q 5, monopolizing the center and leaving Black with a sadly cramped game.

4.	Kt × P	Kt—B 3

Black develops with gain of time, as he is attacking the King Pawn.

5.	Kt—Q B 3	... ...

White also develops with gain of time, protecting the King Pawn.

5.	... ...	P—Q 3

Preparing for the eventual development of his Queen Bishop and also reinforcing his hold on his K 4 square, one of the most valuable center squares.

The customary continuation for White is now the development of his King Bishop: 6 B—K 2.

Instead, White selects an inexact move which results in a complicated game.

6. B—K 3   Kt—K Kt 5!?

This move is open to the objection that it is the second move of the Knight in the opening. Such partiality is always suspicious when—as here—the other player is ahead in development.

Diagram 34

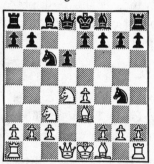

Black's last move poses problems

Black's justification for the Knight's second move is that it creates an embarrassing problem for White. If he retreats his Bishop (say 7 B—B 1), there follows 7 ... Q—Kt 3; attacking White's Knight at his Q 4 square. This Knight would be unable to retreat: if, for example, 8 Kt × Kt??, Q × B P mate!

7.   B—Q B 4!?   ... ...

As will be seen, this move creates a serious weakness in White's Pawn position. However, White further increases his lead in development, which reinforces his confidence in his attacking chances.

7.	... ...	Kt × B
8.	P × B	... ...

Diagram 35

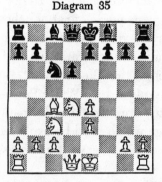

White's position: strong or weak?

Here is an extremely instructive position, for each player has markedly contrasting advantages.

First let us examine White's side of the argument. He has three pieces developed to Black's single piece. So White has a definite plus in development.

Note also that White's Bishop bears down on Black's proverbially weak K B 2 square. Here is a potential source of attacking strength.

This attacking possibility becomes still more potent in view of White's open King Bishop file—which became open in consequence of the Pawn capture on his last move.

To sum up: White's advantages are all tactical advantages: superior development, strong diagonal, open King Bishop file.

Now for Black's assets. He has a superb object of attack in White's doubled and isolated King Pawns. These Pawns are incapable of defending each other. They are static and permanent weaknesses, requiring defense by pieces. There need be no hurry about attacking these weaknesses, as they cannot be dissolved or exchanged. Hence Black can afford to be patient in maneuvering to attack these weaknesses.

The weak Pawns yield Black an extra dividend in the form of a magnificent square at his K 4 for his Knight. Once established at this effective central post, the Knight can never be dislodged by a White Pawn—another consequence of White's crippled Pawn formation. Again, this is not an advantage which need be exploited hurriedly. The Knight can play to K 4, leave it as necessary, return at a later time, etc.

Black has still another advantage in his Bishop-pair. This likewise is an advantage which does not have to be utilized hurriedly. It is an advantage which is dynamic, and can be held in reserve for a long time without forfeiting its effectiveness.

One more asset of Black's position needs mentioning. It is true that momentarily, Black's K B 2 is weak; looks weak; may become weak. But Black can derive consolation from the fact that he has not played ... P—K 4. If he plays ... P—K 3, he will break the diagonal of White's Bishop, and considerably reduce White's attacking chances.

Thus we see that White, who is burdened with a long-term weakness, has only short-term advantages. Black, whose only minus is a somewhat slow development, has a brilliant future based on solid (lasting) positional advantages.

If White is to make the most of his ephemeral advantages, he must hurry, before Black consolidates. But, contrariwise, Black should not hurry to exploit his advantages: they are permanent, inherent in the very nature of the position. Hence the indicated procedure for Black is to defer the realization of his positional advantages until he has first caught up in development and, generally speaking, neutralized White's transitory advantages.

8. ... ...   Kt—K 4

This involves no loss of time, as White's Bishop is menaced. Also his K B 2 square receives additional protection.

9. B—Kt 3   ... ...

Naturally he wants to keep the Bishop on the aggressive diagonal.

Diagram 36

Black's first momentous decision

Black must now decide on the method of developing his King Bishop. He can play ... P—K 3 followed by ... B—K 2; which is safe but slow, or he can play ... P—K Kt 3 followed by ... B—Kt 2 or even ... B—R 3; which is more aggressive but risky. Merely to reflect on these adjectives tells us that the first method is the one in keeping with the proper policy to be pursued by Black.

There is also this important point: by playing 9 ... P—K 3; Black accomplishes two important results: he breaks the diagonal of White's Bishop, so that his K B 2 square is no longer vulnerable. And in addition, he makes it impossible for White to play Kt—Q 5.

The desirability of these two objectives is beyond question. In return for a *permanent* weakness, White has *temporary* advantages, of mobility, of aggressive placement. Let Black wipe out these *temporary* advantages; then he can exploit *his* advantages in all leisure and security, while White is helpless to lift a finger by way of resistance or diversionary counterplay.

9.	P—K Kt 3

Black chooses the livelier and more aggressive line, which at the very least makes his task more difficult. Of course, such choices are often a matter of temperament and taste: to subdue our *subjective* preferences in favor of the *objectively* best course, is often quite difficult.

10. Castles	B—R 3

And here again Black's impatience is noticeable. The more patient and safer course is 10 ... B—Kt 2. As Black plays, he will soon find that *he is combining defense with an attempt to exploit White's positional weaknesses.* This form of gambling fits White's circumstances perfectly, but it is foolhardy on Black's part: it introduces a complicating element which makes Black's technical task much more difficult than it need have been.

11. Kt—Q 5 ... ...

This aggressive move has been made possible by Black's earlier omission of ... P—K 3.

Diagram 37

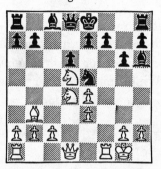

White exploits the omission of ... P—K 3

The average player rarely realizes that one of the ways in which two Bishops prove superior to a Bishop and Knight is that the Knight's mobility can be reduced by judicious Pawn moves. Thus, by playing ... P—K 3 earlier, Black would have cut down the mobility of White's Knights to a very considerable extent. They could never have been able to participate in a King-side attack with the effectiveness they will soon be displaying in the actual game.

11. ... ... **Castles**

12. Q—K 1! ... ...

A good move. White's Queen is about to take up a very aggressive post.

12. ... ... **P—R 4**

Waste of time, as ... P—R 5 is not a real threat. Had Black played ... B—Kt 2 instead of ... B—R 3, he could now drive away the Knight with 12 ... P—K 3.

But, as the position stands, 12 ... P—K 3 is answered by 13 Kt—B 6 ch, K—Kt 2; 14 Q—Kt 3, with a fine attacking game for White.

And so the rather meaningless 12 ... P—R 4 is no more than an expression of bewilderment on Black's part. Again we see how wrong it was for Black to mingle tactical ideas with strategy. White, on the other hand, revels in this opportunity to create complications.

13.   Q—R 4!   ... ...

Diagram 38

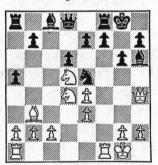

Another inexactitude is punished

At first sight it seems that 13 ... B—Kt 2 is feasible, for after 14 Kt × P ch, K—R 1; there is an awkward pin on White's advanced Knight.

But White has better: 13 ... B—Kt 2; 14 Q × K P!, P—R 5; 15 Q × Q!, R × Q; 16 Kt—Kt 6! In that case, White wins either the Exchange or a second Pawn.

Thus Black is punished for having played the risky 10 ... B—R 3 instead of the safe 10 ... B—Kt 2.

| 13. ... ... | K—Kt 2 |
| 14. Kt × P! | ... ... |

This is possible because if 14 ... P—K Kt 4??; White checks with either Knight at K B 5 and wins at once.

| 14. ... ... | B × P ch |

Black has won the weak Pawn after all, but this is a minor triumph. The Pawn should have been won in a much safer manner after due preparation. Here the win of the Pawn is merely part of some tactical fireworks that are just what White wants.

| 15. K—R 1 | ... ... |

Diagram 39

The crisis!

And here we have the critical position.

Our first impression is that White has blundered, for Black can now win a piece with 15 ... B × Kt. But in that case White has a perpetual check with 16 Q—B 6 ch, K—R 3; 17 Q—R 4 ch, K—Kt 2; 18 Q—B 6 ch, etc.

Black is obviously dissatisfied with this outcome, which is all he deserves after his inexact opening play. He looks for a different method.

For example, suppose he tries 15 ... P—B 3; when both Knights are under attack? If then 16 Kt × B, Black does not play 16 ... Q × Kt? or 16 ... R × Kt?? because of the forking check 17 Kt—K 6 ch. Instead, he plays (after 15 ... P—B 3; 16 Kt × B) 16 ... B × Kt!; and Black's other Knight is trapped!

But White does not allow himself to be thrust back so easily. (See Diagram 39.) In the event of 15 ... P—B 3; he plays 16 Kt/K 7—B 5 ch!, taking advantage of the exposed state of Black's King due to his previous inexact play. If then 16 ... P × Kt; 17 Q—Kt 3 ch. Now on 17 ... Kt—Kt 5; White continues 18 Kt × P ch, regaining the piece in a highly advantageous manner. And on 17 ... B—Kt 4; there follows 18 P—K R 4!, P × P; 19 P × B, P × P; 20 R × R, K × R; 21 R—K B 1 ch, K—Kt 2; 22 B—K 6!, and White's terrific attacking position is well worth two Pawns.

Thus we see that Black's inexact play has permitted White to assemble a wealth of tactical resources. The sensible conclusion for Black, then, is to recognize the defeat of his policy and permit the perpetual check which ensues after 15 ... B × Kt.

But Black is headstrong, and insists on carrying out his faulty plan to the bitter end.

| 15. | ... ... | Kt—Kt 5? |

(See Diagram 40)

| 16. | Kt/Q 4—B 5 ch! | ... ... |

Diagram 40

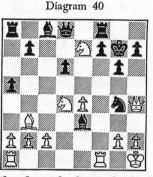

What has Black overlooked?

This clever sacrifice, made possible by Black's previous faulty play, definitely removes the game's strategical content and transfers it to an exclusively tactical sphere. But this is highly advantageous for White!

16. ... ...   P × Kt

17. P × P   ... ...

With his Knight *en prise*, his King exposed, and his Bishop on K 6 loose in some variations, Black is beginning to pay the penalty for his earlier sins. Each of them was minor in itself; but cumulatively they add up to defeat.

Diagram 41

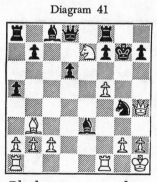

Black is in a quandary

The position is baffling for Black.

If he plays 17 ... Kt—B 3; then 18 Q—Kt 3 ch, K—R 1; 19 Q × B, R—K 1; 20 Q R—K 1 gives White a winning position.

If instead 17 ... Kt—B 7 ch; 18 R × Kt, B × R; 19 Q—Kt 5 ch, K—R 1; 20 Q—B 6 mate!

Again, if 17 ... Kt—R 3; 18 P—B 6 ch, K—R 1; 19 Q R—K 1, Kt—Kt 5; 20 R × B, Kt × R; 21 Q—R 6 (threatens mate), K R—Kt 1; 22 B × P, and Black is lost.

17.	... ...	K—R 1
18.	B × P!?	... ...

This is rubbing it in. So faulty has Black's play been that his K B 2 square has turned out to be a weakness after all!

Alas, Black cannot play 18 ... R × B?; because of 19 Kt—Kt 6 ch winning the Queen!

However, White's simplest course was 18 Q R—K 1, for example 18 ... P—B 3; 19 Q × Kt, Q × Kt; 20 R—B 3 winning easily.

Diagram 42

Can Black defend himself?

In the position of Diagram 42, Black might try 18 ...
B—R 3. Then if 19 Q R—K 1, B—Q 2 (threatening to
capture the Bishop); 20 B—Q 5, Kt—K 4; 21 Q × B,
Q × Kt; 22 P—B 6 still wins for White.

Note that after 18 ... B—R 3; 19 Q R—K 1, B—Kt 2??;
allows 20 Kt—Kt 6 mate!

The best chance, albeit a losing one, is 18 ... B—R 3;
19 Q R—K 1, B—Q 2; 20 B—Q 5, B × P. Then, after 21
R × B, R × R; 22 Kt × R, Q × Q; 23 Kt × Q, Black will
lose the endgame.

18.	Q—Kt 3

This removal of the Queen is equivalent to resignation.

Diagram 43

White must win

A neat winning line for White is 19 Kt—Kt 6 ch, K—
Kt 2; 20 P—B 6 ch, K × B; 21 Q × P ch, K—K 3; 22 Kt ×
R ch, with an easy victory in sight.

19. Q × Kt	... ...

Also good enough. If now 19 ... B—Q 2; 20 Q—R 5 wins
easily.

19. ... ...   **R × B?**

Demoralization.

20. Q—Kt 8 mate

SUMMARY: White consistently played his trumps (tactical play). Black, on the other hand, foolishly neglected his indicated course (patient, quiet position play), and mistakenly accepted White's desperate invitation to a complicated struggle. Black lost the game by failing to fight on terrain of his own choosing. The variations (giving possible lines of play which did not actually occur) are extremely instructive, and should be studied with the greatest care.

VIII

Plan from the Start

THE average player always has an uneasy feeling that he "ought to learn the openings." He thinks of "the openings" as a systematically arranged body of knowledge, like the Code of Justinian or the Periodic Table of the elements.

That is one aspect, it is true, of the openings. They can be found in such compilations as *Modern Chess Openings,* which bristles formidably with more than a thousand columns of opening play, with thousands of alternative lines. But "the openings" are less important than "the opening."

It is "the opening" that interests us. When the master plays his opening moves, he selects them on the basis of some plan he has in mind. Where this prior consideration is not present, the reverse process takes place in his mind. He plays this or that opening on the spur of the moment, or improvises as conditions require. But, assuming he does not start with a prior plan, *he soon evolves a plan from the unforeseen moves he is making.* The play which is to take place in the middle game already exists in embryo in the opening.

There may be some initial resistance on your part to this notion. Take the first game in this book (page 13). The play is strictly on a move-to-move basis, with no thought of planning. That game is the first one in the book for precisely that reason: *chess without planning is chess on its most elementary level.* But we have now advanced beyond that stage, and we are ready to scrutinize opening moves for whatever hints they may give us about the future course of the game.

The most useful source of information about the coming trend of the game is the Pawn configuration. (This one point is the most important sentence in the whole book!) Just as the scientist can reconstruct the complete skeleton of a prehistoric monster from a heap of bone fragments, the master who studies the Pawn configuration can see his plans neatly prepared for him.

To the average player this concept may seem fantastic because of its novelty and implausibility. But in the remaining games, we shall apply this guiding idea again and again, and always with useful conclusions. For once planning becomes possible, an individual game is no longer like one of those Foreign Legion duels fought in the dark with knives and lanterns. Your games will be just as exciting as they ever were, but you will have a satisfying feeling that the chessmen are truly under your control. Games that are jumbled, with a hit-or-miss, helter-skelter character, can be very exciting. They can also be very depressing.

But once the element of planning appears, your games take on a more satisfying quality because they give scope to your creative abilities. Now let us put these theories to the test.

King Fianchetto Defense

White	Black
1. P—K 4	P—K Kt 3

Now here is a move which speaks volumes. In the first six games, Black answered 1 P—K 4 with ... P—K 4, to foster his development and have a firm foothold in the center. In the seventh game, Black replied 1 ... P—Q B 4, still bearing down on White's Q 4 square and thus fighting for his fair share of the center.

But 1 ... P—K Kt 3 is a different kind of move. It provides for the "fianchetto" of Black's King Bishop (... B—Kt 2) and is therefore a developing move of sorts.

Nevertheless, 1 ... P—K Kt 3 has a serious flaw: *it does not fight for the center.* For what is to hinder White from now playing 2 P—Q 4, setting up a monopolistic Pawn center?

2. P—Q 4	... ...

Of course. White seizes the opportunity to establish an overwhelming Pawn center.

Diagram 44

Black is condemned to a constricted game

White has played up both center Pawns without opposition. We know even at this early stage, when the game has barely started, that White will be able to develop his pieces aggressively, effortlessly.

And Black? His game is bound to be constricted. He has no foothold in the center; hence he cannot establish his pieces in that most vital sector. If he plays ... Kt—K B 3, the Knight is kicked away by P—K 5. If he plays ... Kt—Q B 3, *that* Knight is driven off by P—Q 5. It is clear that Black's chances of getting a promising, effective development are hopeless.

Even at this point, the game is no longer a formless gamble: the Pawn configuration has given us the information about the future course of the game!

| 2. | ... ... | B—Kt 2 |
| 3. | P—K B 4 | ... ... |

White reinforces his hold on the center.

| 3. | ... ... | P—Kt 3 |

The other Bishop is to be fianchettoed as well.

| 4. | Kt—K B 3 | B—Kt 2 |
| 5. | B—Q 3 | ... ... |

White's development is natural, powerful. Black's pieces have little scope, and the problem of how to develop his Knights becomes more acute with every move.

| 5. | ... ... | Kt—Q B 3 |

White can drive this Knight with 6 P—Q 5; instead, he prefers a solid move which fortifies his Pawn center.

| 6. | P—B 3 | P—K 3 |

Possibly with a view to playing ... Kt/B 3—K 2 in case his Queen Knight is attacked by P—Q 5. As the game continues, the original diagnosis is confirmed: Black's game is painfully constricted, and no rational course of action is available to him. White has a lasting initiative.

>   **7.   B—K 3   Kt—R 3**

A Knight is always posted poorly at the side of the board, as the number of squares to which he has access is smaller than when he is located in the center or near the center.

>   **8.   P—K R 3!   ... ...**

Diagram 45

White combines constriction with attack

White's last move is a good one on two counts. In the first place, it prevents any disturbance by a possible ... Kt—K Kt 5. (We have already seen—page 82—that one of the most effective procedures against a Knight is to cut down the number of squares available to him.)

The other useful aspect of 8 P—K R 3! is that it is a preparation for a general Pawn advance which may involve P—K Kt 4 and eventually P—K R 4—K R 5. This will be useful both for attacking purposes and also to cramp Black's position even more severely.

8.	... ...	**Castles**
9.	**P—K Kt 4**	... ...

So pitiable is the immobility of Black's pieces that this move actually threatens to win a piece by P—Kt 5.

9.	... ...	**P—B 3**

He creates a retreat for his menaced King Knight, but in so doing, he buries his King Bishop. This sort of thing is characteristic of such crowded positions: every plus, of even the most trivial kind, can only be purchased by a greater minus.

10.	**Q—K 2**	... ...

White has formulated his plan of attack, which will be explained concretely a few moves later. Meanwhile he develops more pieces in order to lend full force to the attack when it does come into being.

10.	... ...	**Kt—B 2**

There does not seem to be much point to this move, but Black is not in a position to make significant moves.

11.	**Q Kt—Q 2**	... ...

And still White continues with his sound development, steadily gaining in power. The development of White's pieces reminds us of a hearty extrovert, glowing with health and good spirits. The state of Black's colorless and cramped game invokes the spirit of ulcers and migraine headaches.

11.	Kt—K 2

Another regrouping move; in an unsatisfactory situation, regrouping moves are the order of the day, if only because they imply a fussy feeling of activity in a position which offers no scope for active play.

However, there is one feature of Black's last move which merits White's attention: the diagonal of Black's Queen Bishop has been unmasked. An experienced player would make a mental note of the fact that White's King Rook is at the tail end of this diagonal. If tactical complications arise later on, the fact that there is a potential target on the long diagonal may complicate matters for White. At present, no danger is involved.

12. P—K R 4!	... ...

Diagram 46

White intends to storm the hostile castled position

At this point it will be useful to review what we learned in the sixth game (page 61) about creating open lines for attack on the castled position. We saw that once one of the Pawns in front of the castled King advances to the third rank, the aggressor has a relatively easy time opening a file by advancing his own Pawns and forcing a file open by Pawn exchanges.

This is precisely what White has in mind: he intends to open the King Rook file by playing P—R 5. With this file opened, he will have access to the Black King. And with Black's position as cramped as it is, his chances of success-ful defense are infinitesimal.

Here we have White's plan in its final form. Some of it has been foreshadowed as early as the second move; but now we have reached a point where it is concrete and about to be fulfilled.

The crucial question is: will the execution be on the same high level of the planning?

12.   ... ...   P—Q 4

At last, after so much preliminary fumbling and aim-less fidgeting, Black makes a belated struggle for control of the center. And, strangely enough, with all the keys to victory in his hands, White seems to be disconcerted!

Diagram 47

The critical point

Once more we are confronted with the (chiefly psychological) problem of recognizing that a crisis is at hand.

If White realizes that Black wants to play ... P × P to achieve the only slight measure of freedom he can hope for, then White's reply is clearly indicated: 13 P—K 5! Here is the reasoning behind that move:

When you have your opponent trussed up, your main object must be to keep him in that state. All attempts at freedom, unless they can be definitely stopped, must be prevented. By playing 13 P—K 5!, White closes the center files and the diagonals; he virtually deprives Black's four minor pieces of mobility and hence counterplay; and finally he still retains the possibility of opening a file for attacking Black's King.

| 13. | P—R 5? | ... ... |

Premature, hence faulty execution of his plan. Now Black, despite the continuing miserable appearance of his game, obtains real counterplay.

| 13. | ... ... | Q P × P |

Now at least the Queen Bishop has some scope.

| 14. | P × P | ... ... |

This and the following exchanges are questionable, as they lead to a clearly lost game for White on move 19.

| 14. | ... ... | Kt × P |

Now the position of this Knight is greatly improved. As against this, White has opened the King Rook file, with a number of threats, such as Q—R 2.

| 15. | Kt × P | P—K B 4 |

Diagram 48

Black fights back!

Black is hitting back as best he can. Note how the character of his play has changed, now that his pieces have some scope for action.

White can play 16 Q—R 2 (threatening mate), but after 16 ... Kt—R 3 the situation is unclear, primarily because of White's somewhat precarious position on the long diagonal.

16.	P × P	... ...

This exchange is unavoidable, but now the King file is opened, and we suddenly realize that White has not castled, and that his King and Queen are on the same file, vulnerable to a pin. Had White played 13 P—K 5!, this danger would never have materialized.

16.	... ...	P × P
17.	Kt/K 4—Kt 5	Kt × Kt
18.	P × Kt	P—B 5!

Well played! Once the attacked Bishop retreats, Black can play 19 ... R—K 1 with a winning game!

Diagram 49

Black has the initiative!

There can no longer be any doubt that White has botched the task of cashing in on his advantage. If he tries 19 Q—R 2, Black can calmly reply 19 ... R—K 1!; 20 Q × P ch, K—B 1; and White's position, with two pieces *en prise*, is more shaky than Black's!

But White still has a tactical resource, whereby he tries to turn the opening-up of the position to his own advantage.

19.   B—B 4 ch!   ... ...

This produces a second crisis, and now Black is subjected to the stern test of having to realize that his reply will decide the fate of the game.

(*See Diagram 50*)

The right move for Black is 19 ... B—Q 4! Then if 20 B—Q 2, R—K 1; 21 Kt—K 5, Kt × Kt; and White is quite lost, as after 22 P × Kt, R × P; he loses the Queen because of the pin on the King file. It is indeed a pity that this is not the actual conclusion of the game: logic as well as

Diagram 50

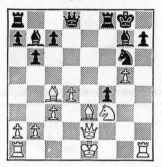

How should the check be answered?

---

aesthetics require that White should be punished incisively for his faulty execution of a first-rate plan.

	19.	K—R 1??

Quite certain of victory, Black is actually committing suicide!

	20.	B—Q 2	R—K 1
	21.	Kt—K 5!	... ...

Diagram 51

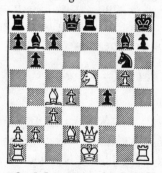

Black has miscalculated!

Now Black suddenly discovers, to his consternation, that he has overlooked a tactical fine point: if 21 ... Kt × Kt; 22 R × P ch!! (triumph of the open King Rook file!), K × R; 23 Q—R 5 ch, B—R 3; 24 Q × B mate.

Likewise, if 21 ... B × Kt; 22 R × P ch!!, K × R; 23 Q—R 5 ch, K—Kt 2; 24 Q—R 6 mate.

| 21. | ... ... | B × R |

Hopeless, for now he loses his Queen.

22.	Kt—B 7 ch	K—Kt 1
23.	Kt × Q dis ch	K—B 1
24.	Kt—K 6 ch	K—Kt 1

With Queen for Rook and plenty of unspent attacking force, White wins as he pleases.

| 25. | Castles | P—B 6 |
| 26. | Q—K 4 | K—R 1 |

If 26 ... B—Kt 7; 27 Kt × P dis ch with disastrous consequences for Black.

| 27. | R × B | Resigns |

SUMMARY: White planned the game admirably, but his execution was faulty because he failed to recognize the crisis when it arrived. Thereafter Black freed himself move by move until *he* had a won game; but at the second crisis, he too missed the proper continuation. This is the kind of game of which the loser says, "I had him on the ropes but I let him get away." This is not a matter of "bad luck." It is a matter of not following through consistently; of not rising to the occasion; of weakening just when one final, conclusive effort is required. In chess, the only victory is total victory.

IX

Exploit Weak Color Complexes

WHEN Virgil speaks of rocks crying out (*saxa clamant*), we accept the idea indulgently as part of the poet's stock-in-trade. But when we say that squares may be weak, the expression sounds silly as part of the exposition of a semi-scientific subject. Yet it is a fact that squares on the chessboard can be weak. This is best explained by example.

In Diagram 53, we observe that the following squares in Black's camp are weak: Q 3 and K B 3. Why? *Because these squares are no longer commanded by Black Pawns.* Such squares are known as "holes." They are gaps in the Pawn configuration into which the enemy pieces can infiltrate. If these squares were still protected by Black Pawns, they would not be holes, and they would be safe from hostile invasion.

Suppose, for example, that in Diagram 53 Black's King Pawn were still at his K 2 square. In that event, the King Pawn would protect Black's Q 3 and K B 3 squares; they would not be holes; they would not be susceptible to invasion by White.

There are several types of positions in which holes are

relatively bearable. Where the player thus afflicted still
has the Bishop which moves on the color of the weak
squares, the Bishop provides a certain amount of protection for them. (In Diagram 53, Black has weak black
squares; but he still has his King Bishop, which moves on
black squares and can therefore play a valuable defensive
role.)

Again, if the opponent lacks the Bishop which travels
on the color of the weak squares, the possibility of exploiting the weakness likewise diminishes. (In Diagram 53,
White has his Queen Bishop, which may be expected to
do some effective work on the weakened black squares.)

Holes are also relatively bearable where the position is
closed. If the aggressor does not have free access (through
open files and diagonals) to the weakened squares, it
stands to reason that their weakness is minimized. (That is
why, in Diagram 53, White immediately plays 5 P—Q 4!,
opening up the position to gain access to the weakened
squares.)

The weakness of holes becomes particularly critical
when the opponent has one or more Knights. The reason
for this is most interesting. An individual Bishop commands squares of only one color. If the attacker has only
the "wrong" Bishop, the holes are immune from occupation by that Bishop. But a Knight can reach squares of
either color; so, with a Knight available, the attacker is
bound to occupy the hole sooner or later. The following
game is particularly instructive on this point, because once
White's Knight occupies the hole at his Q 6 square, the
paralyzing effect is felt throughout the Black camp.

One final point: the concept of weak squares seems a
bit on the esoteric side, because, although it has played

a vital role in master chess for at least the past fifty years, it has been deemed too "highbrow" for books of instruction. To know how to exploit weak squares is, however, definitely useful to the ordinary player, because this type of weakness is particularly likely to occur in the play of his opponents.

The exploitation of weak squares requires a technique which is easily understood, easily mastered, and easily applied.

Sicilian Defense

White	Black
1. P—K 4	P—Q B 4
2. Kt—K B 3	Kt—Q B 3
3. P—B 4	... ...

This move is somewhat questionable, as it creates a hole at White's Q 4 square. (That square is no longer guarded by either White's King Pawn or Queen Bishop Pawn.) However, the square, although now a hole, is amply guarded by White's Knight on his K B 3 square.

Diagram 52

White's Q 4 square is a hole

If Black tries to exploit the fact that White's Q 4 square is a hole by occupying it with his Knight, he gets nowhere: 3 ... Kt—Q 5; 4 Kt × Kt, P × Kt; and the hole has actually disappeared!

From this we derive an important rule: don't occupy a weak square in the enemy's camp unless you can recapture *with a piece*. This type of recapture permits you to continue exploiting the weakness. Recapture with a Pawn simply plugs up the gap. Pawn captures, we have learned, create open lines; but on occasion, Pawn captures can close lines as well.

3.	P—K 3

This move creates a hole at Black's Q 3 square which may become a troublesome weakness. Hence 3 ... P—Q 3 is safer; it avoids this organic weakness.

4. Kt—B 3	... ...

More logical is the immediate 4 P—Q 4, opening up the position and therefore facilitating the exploitation of Black's hole at his Q 3 square.

4.	P—K Kt 3??

This is a serious strategical blunder. Black already has a hole at his Q 3 square; now he creates another hole at his K B 3 square.

(*See Diagram 53*)

5. P—Q 4!	... ...

Quite right. He opens up the position in order to bear down on the weak squares in Black's camp.

Diagram 53

Black's position is seriously weakened

5.	... ...	P × P
6.	Kt × P	... ...

Black's strategical *faux pas* has already condemned him to a permanently difficult position. His best course is perhaps 6 ... P—Q R 3, in order to prevent the following Knight maneuver.

| 6. | ... ... | B—Kt 2? |

Having played ... P—K Kt 3, it is natural enough for him to fianchetto the Bishop; but now his Q 3 square is deprived of protection by this Bishop.

| 7. | Kt/Q 4—Kt 5! | ... ... |

The indicated move, and a very powerful one. The Knight is about to occupy the hole at White's Q 6 square (Black's Q 3 square); and there is nothing that Black can do about it.

It is highly instructive to observe the consequences of this maneuver: one evil leads to another, and Black's game goes inexorably downhill.

7.   ... ...   K Kt—K 2

Black would like to castle; but White puts in a veto.

8.   Kt—Q 6 ch   ... ...

Diagram 54

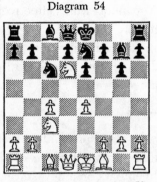

The hole is occupied!

Now Black's King must move, and he can never castle.
The King will be in lasting danger, his King Rook will
never be properly developed; the Queen Bishop's possibilities of development are dim indeed. And so the disastrous sequel to the weakening of Black's Q 3 square has its
dismal unfolding.

8.   ... ...   K—B 1
9.   P—B 4   ... ...

An excellent, aggressive move: it prepares for reinforce-
ment of the Knight by P—K 5, or for line-opening with
P—B 5. The choice of alternatives will be dictated by the
further course of the game.

9.   ... ...   P—Kt 3

A shy attempt to develop the Queen Bishop. Of this

attempt we need say no more, beyond remarking that this Bishop is on his home square at the end of the game!

10.   B—K 2   Kt—Q 5

Black embarks on what is *theoretically* sound policy. Unfortunately it cannot work effectively in a position which is theoretically unsound!

The intention is to exchange some pieces and thus ease Black's cramped game. But Black's positional minus is so great that exchanges are no help.

11.   B—K 3   ... ...

White calmly develops piece after piece, secure in the knowledge that his preponderance of development will soon allow him to embark on a devastatingly active course.

Diagram 55

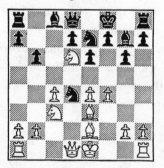

Has White violated the principle
of quick development?

Since we have raised the subject of development, this is an appropriate point to inquire: how about the White Knight maneuver from K B 3 to Q 4 to Q Kt 5 to Q 6? Wasn't that waste of time? Doesn't it violate the rule against moving the same piece too often in the opening? How do you get good results from violation of sound principle?

These are good questions, and require careful study of the situation.

The first move of White's Knight (2 Kt—K B 3) was not waste of time, as it was a natural developing move.

The recapture on White's Q 4 square (6 Kt × P) was not waste of time, as it was made in reply to a Black move (5 ... P × P) which certainly contributed nothing of value to Black's position. In addition, the move of White's Knight from K B 3 to Q 4 brought it to a more useful and aggressive post.

As for 7 Kt/Q 4—Kt 5!, it was a technical violation of the rules of good development; but the good elements of this move outweigh by far its academic drawback. The permanent occupation of White's Q 6 square is such a tremendous asset that the mere waste of one move shrinks to nothingness in comparison.

The same argument applies to 8 Kt—Q 6 ch, aside from the fact that it forces a reply (8 ... K—B 1), which is not only useless for Black, but directly harmful for him.

At this point, it can be revealed that the rule against moving the same piece repeatedly does not have quite the same stringency as one of the Ten Commandments. In beginners' games, the *aimless* repeated moving of the same piece is a serious handicap which leads to many a lost game. It is therefore necessary, at the start, to prohibit such repeated moves in harsh and categorical language. As a player improves, however, his position judgment becomes more reliable. He can be trusted to know when such repeated moves are permissible. They are unobjectionable, and even quite powerful, when there is a good, constructive reason for them, or when they are sanctioned by prior transgressions on the enemy's part.

11.   ... ...   Kt × B
12.   Q × Kt   ... ...

White has developed four pieces, Black has only two pieces out. White's forces function effectively and their potential powers are considerable. By no stretch of the imagination can one anticipate any great activity for the Black pieces.

Diagram 56

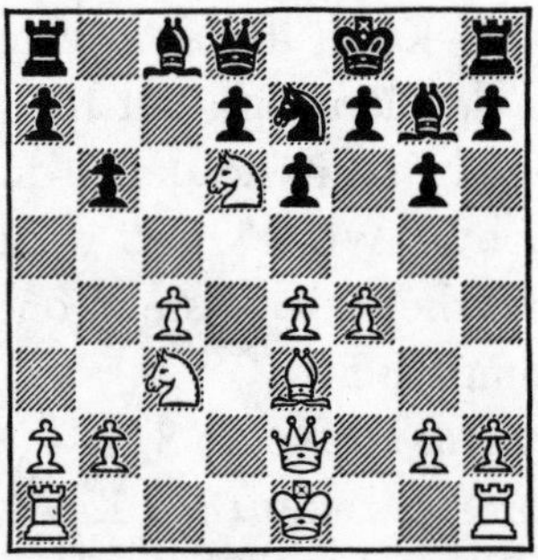

Black blunders

12.   ... ...   B × Kt ch?

A strategical blunder of the first magnitude. Black voluntarily deprives himself of the best protection for his denuded black squares. In the absence of the Bishop, the weakness of the black squares is so pitilessly underlined that what started out as a strategical weakness becomes also a tactical weakness. White soon works up an attack which rides roughshod over these weak squares.

13. P × B   ... ...

It is true that White's Queen Bishop Pawns are isolated and doubled—a classic weakness (see page 170 for a discussion of this theme.) But circumstances alter cases, especially in chess. White's "weakness" is not really a weakness because Black is in no condition to take advantage of it. This is borne out by the fact that the state of these Pawns is at no time an issue during the rest of the game.

13. ... ...   **Kt—B 3**
14. P—K B 5!   ... ...

Played with splendid judgment. The opening of attacking lines always favors the player with the better development; the more superior his development, the more powerful his attack.

Diagram 57

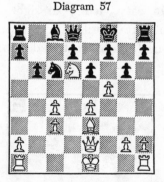

White's attack begins!

Black must submit to the opening of at least one file. With his King in danger and his development in arrears, he has no hope of weathering the storm.

Here is one possibility: 14 ... K P × P; 15 P × P, Q—B 3; 16 Castles!—for if 16 ... Q × Kt; 17 B—R 6 ch, K—Kt 1; 18 Q—K 8 ch (the effects of line-opening become noticeable!), Q—B 1; 19 Q × Q mate.

14. ... ...   **Q—B 3**

There is a slightly better defense in 14 ... K—Kt 2— but not enough to matter.

15.   Castles K R!   ... ...

Threatening 16 P × K P or 16 P × Kt P with a crushing attack on the newly opened King Bishop file.

15. ... ...   **K P × P**

White has many pretty winning lines hereabouts, for example: 15 ... P—K 4; 16 Kt × P!, K × Kt; 17 P × P ch—or 15 ... P—K 4; 16 Kt × P!, Q × Kt; 17 P × P, etc. In either case White wins the Queen for a Rook and Knight, with an easy victory in sight because Black's King remains in mortal peril and can expect no assistance worth mentioning from his scattered associates.

Diagram 58

White's Knight is attacked

16.   P × P!   ... ...

In a fine position, it is easy to be brilliant. If now 16
... Q × Kt; 17 B—R 6 ch leads to mate, as previously
shown.

The shocking weakness of his black squares does not
leave Black much choice. If he tries to prevent B—R 6
ch by playing 16 ... P—K R 4; there follows 17 P × P!
(the line-opening is always decisive!), Q × Kt; 18 B—R
6 ch!!, R × B; 19 R × P ch, K—Kt 1; 20 Q—K 8 ch and
mate next move.

And finally, if 16 ... B—R 3 (in order to guard against
the eventual Q—K 8 ch), there is an easy win after 17
B—R 6 ch, K—Kt 1; 18 Kt—K 4.

I. 18 ... Q—R 5; 19 B—Kt 5, Q—R 4; 20 Kt—B 6 ch
forking King and Queen.

II. 18 ... Q—K 2; 19 P × P, B P × P; 20 Kt—B 6 ch,
K—B 2; 21 Kt—Q 5 dis ch winning the Queen.

III. 18 ... Q—K 4; 19 P × P, P—B 4; 20 R × P!!, Q
× R; 21 R—K B 1, Q × P; 22 Q—B 3! and now White
threatens 23 Q—B 8 ch! followed by mate. If 22 ... Q × B;
23 Q—B 7 mate.

Thus White drives home the attack on the weak black
squares and the open King Bishop file.

16.   ... ...   **P—K Kt 4**

(*See Diagram* 59)

17.   Kt—K 4!   ... ...

White now wins the King Knight Pawn, smashing
Black's last bulwark.

17.   ... ...   **Q—Kt 2**

Diagram 59

Black tries to close the attacking lines

Equally hopeless is 17 ... Q—K 4; 18 B × K Kt P, K R—Kt 1; 19 B—B 6, Q—B 2; 20 Q R—K 1, etc.

18. B × K Kt P   ... ...

Threatening (among other things) 19 B—B 6, winning the Exchange. Always the same motif: White has a field day on the enfeebled black squares.

18.	... ...	K R—Kt 1
19.	Kt—B 6!	... ...

Diagram 60

White's attack rolls on

The immediate threat is 20 Q—K 8 mate.

If 19 ... B—R 3; 20 Kt × Q P mate.

If 19 ... Q × B; 20 Kt × R P ch forking Black's King and Queen.

19.	... ...	Kt—K 2
20.	Kt × Q P ch!	B × Kt
21.	Q × Kt mate	

SUMMARY: Black weakened his black squares and then deprived them of what scanty protection they enjoyed. White concentrated on this weakness, obtained a tremendous lead in development, opened lines for his vastly more mobile pieces, and scored a quick, incisive victory. It should be added that the exploitation of weak squares is usually a strategical problem. In this game it took on tactical significance because Black's King was exceptionally vulnerable.

X

Concentrate on Targets in Your Opponent's Castled Position

ANY weakness in your opponent's position is a boon when you are trying to devise a plan. In chess, a weakness serves the same function as a clue in a whodunit. The weakness gives the position character, definition, and clarity. What was opaque becomes transparent. What was impenetrable becomes perfectly obvious.

The weakness gives us our point of departure. Once we recognize it, we know how to proceed. Of course, some weaknesses are easier to exploit than others. But there is nothing esoteric about a weakness in the hostile castled position. We know that the fate of the game depends on the King's security. Hence we know that an attack on that castled position is desirable—*if there is a weakness in the castled position.*

An attack on an unweakened castled position is chancy, very likely futile. Not so when a weakness exists in the castled position. For then the probabilities of success are greatly enhanced. And if the attacker has a good, aggressive development, while the defender has a cramped, listless development, the likelihood of success is correspondingly enhanced still more.

But, having profited by the initial hint of the weakness, we benefit still more as we proceed. To exploit the hostile weakness is the most logical procedure in chess. It is also one of the most enjoyable aspects of the game, for it gives more scope to a player's creative abilities than any other feature of the game. What more concrete proof of ability than to discern an attainable goal, and then operate in such a manner that the goal is achieved, regardless of whatever resistance is offered by the enemy?

There is an added element of enjoyment in the process in that the attack against weaknesses in the castled position often allows the aggressor to indulge in brilliant sacrifices at the decisive moment. The defender, hampered by his weakness and his faulty development, cannot possibly function at the full theoretical level of his playing strength. The qualitative local superiority of the attacker in the critical zone is so great that he can deliberately offer up some of his material and, by a triumph of mind over matter, bring about a decision which is not only quick but also elegant. This produces a feeling of elation that is truly soothing to one's ego; it is one of the major satisfactions which chess is capable of offering to its devotees.

It is one of the most enticing riddles of the centuries-old attractiveness of chess that a phenomenon so deeply rooted in the materialistic and rapacious should offer a satisfaction which is so deeply spiritual and so innocent of harm to one's fellow man!

QUEEN'S GAMBIT DECLINED

White	Black
1. P—Q 4	P—Q 4
2. P—Q B 4	... ...

This is the Queen-side equivalent of the King's Gambit. (See the second game, page 25.) White would like to remove Black's center Pawn, in order to be able to play P—K 4 with a broad, powerful center.

Whereas the King's Gambit involves some danger to White's King because it opens up lines in the King's vicinity, the Queen's Gambit involves no danger to White's King because the line-opening does not take place in the King's vicinity.

Because the Queen's Gambit involves no danger to White's King and because it puts up a strong fight for control of the center, it is one of the most popular openings in modern master play.

2.	P—K 3

Black supports his center Pawn, so that in the event of 3 P × P, he can reply 3 ... P × P; maintaining his hold on the center and restraining White from playing P—K 4.

Diagram 61

Black fights for the center

3.   Kt—K B 3   Kt—K B 3

Playing out the King Knight in this manner is always a good developing move. In this opening the Knight move has an added significance: the Knight's main function is to maintain control of the K 5 square, and in some cases, to occupy it.

Control and/or occupation of the K 5 square is usually a symptom of a very fine position in the Queen Pawn openings. Contrariwise, failure to control this key square is generally symptomatic of a poor or inferior position.

4.   Kt—B 3   P—B 4

This is likewise one of the key moves of the opening. The move of the Queen Bishop Pawn helps Black fight for the center by trying to divert White's Queen Pawn from its control of the K 5 square. Another function of Black's last move is that it may lead to Pawn captures which will result in open files for Black's Rooks.

(It would be quite wrong, in Queen Pawn openings of this character, to play a move like 4 ... Kt—B 3; making it impossible for Black to advance his Queen Bishop Pawn. The distasteful consequences for Black would be that it would be impossible to exert counterpressure against White's Queen Pawn and that it would be next door to impossible to secure an open file for Black's Rooks.)

5.   Q P × P   ... ...

This is feeble. Better is the aggressive developing move 5 B—Kt 5, which, by pinning Black's Knight (and thus paralyzing it temporarily) consistently pursues the theme of fighting for control of the center.

Another good alternative is 5 P—K 3, which also serves a valuable function, in that it enables White to answer a possible ... B P × P with K P × P, still maintaining White's hold on the K 5 square. It is true that 5 P—K 3 has the drawback of hemming in White's Queen Bishop (just as Black's Queen Bishop is at present hemmed in by the Black Pawn at his K 3 square). This is one of the great strategical problems of the Queen Pawn openings: P—K 3 often deprives the Queen Bishop of most of its mobility.

Diagram 62

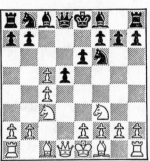

White has weakened his center control

By playing 5 Q P × P, White has weakened his hold on K 5, and made it that much easier for Black to free himself.

5.   ... ...   B × P

The Pawn exchange also merits criticism on this score: whereas 5 Q P × P contributes nothing whatever to White's development, the reply 5 ... B × P brings a Black piece into effective play. Black is already prepared to castle, whereas White still requires two more moves before he can castle.

6. P × P?	... ...

Another error of judgment. The Pawn exchange, like its predecessor, only frees Black's game.

6.	Kt × P

The alternative 6 ... P × P looks attractive, as it opens the diagonal for the free development of Black's Queen Bishop. But White has a formidable reply in 7 B—Kt 5. The point is this: 6 ... P × P results in an isolated Queen Pawn, which, being unguarded by Pawns, must rely on the protection of pieces. But after 7 B—Kt 5, Black's King Knight is deprived of its protective function by reason of the pin. Black therefore rightly prefers the text method of recapture.

7. Kt × Kt	... ...

Still another exchange which frees Black's game! But here the choice was no longer easy.

One's first notion is that 7 P—K 4, Kt × Kt; 8 Q × Q ch, K × Q; 9 P × Kt, is a good line for White, because Black's King has been compelled to move and has thus lost the castling privilege. This is a mistaken idea, however, for once the Queens are exchanged, the tactical danger to the King diminishes considerably, and there is far less need for him to huddle timorously at the side of the board.

Secondly, this series of hypothetical exchanges would result in an isolated Queen Bishop Pawn for White—a serious weakness in the endgame.

7. ... ...   **P × Kt**

The exchanges have wound up with an isolated Queen Pawn for Black after all; but, as he is no longer vulnerable to the pinning move B—Kt 5, he need not worry overmuch about his isolated Pawn.

In any case, the potential weakness of this Pawn is a minor matter in comparison with the freedom Black has acquired through the exchanges.

Diagram 63

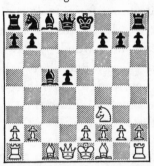

Black's Queen Bishop can develop freely

The most important consequence of the exchanges is that Black now has an open diagonal for his Queen Bishop. This solves the most pressing problem of development with which Black is confronted in this opening.

8. P—K 3   **... ... ...**

It is high time for this move, if White is to be able to develop his King Bishop and then proceed to castle. Nevertheless, White's Queen Bishop is now hemmed in for good.

8. ... ...   **Castles**

Black is already ahead in development. In addition, his pieces will land on better squares, which in turn means that he will have better prospects for aggressive action later on.

It is very important for us to dwell on this point, for it is in this early twilight zone between opening and middle game that the foundation is laid for the subsequent attack. We must think of the game as an integrated whole in which the early shortcomings on White's part are irrevocably linked with White's later impotence in defending his game; otherwise the intervening stage takes on a nebulous, formless appearance and does not make any sense at all. It is this intervening stage that gives the ordinary player so much trouble, because he fails to perceive the connections and consequences.

On the other hand, if we dwell on the individual moves and try to foresee their significance for the later play, we will not be astonished, not to say baffled, at the rapid formation of Black's attack. Black's development is not an end in itself: it is an end which in turn becomes the means to a more definitive end: the unfolding of Black's subsequent attack.

9. B—K 2 ... ...

This modest move shows that there is something rotten in the State of Denmark. Whereas Black's Bishops are able to develop freely, White has to develop his King Bishop defensively. (As for White's Queen Bishop, the development of this piece has to be postponed for the time being.) It would be more aggressive to develop the King Bishop to Q 3, but this would have the double drawback of renouncing any potential pressure on the isolated Queen Pawn and of allowing the annoying pin ... B—K Kt 5.

Thus we see that Black's prospects of aggressive development have an inhibiting effect on White's mode of development.

9.		Kt—B 3

Another good developing move.

10. Castles		... ...

At last White has been able to castle.

10.		R—K 1

The Rook is excellently posted here on the half-open file. And since Black's position is predominantly offensive in character, the Rook move partakes of that offensive character. Already there exists the possibility of ... R—K 3 followed by ... R—K Kt 3 with direct menace aimed at the White King. (Note that this powerful Rook maneuver can terminate at K Kt 3 because White did not feel justified in playing B—Q 3, and contented himself with the more modest B—K 2. Again and again we encounter this thought, that every concession implies still another concession to come; whereas every gain made by Black implies still another gain to come.)

(See Diagram 64)

11. B—Kt 5?		... ...

White's position was already sufficiently compromised not to permit the luxury of second-rate moves. Making a second move with this Bishop is definitely a violation

Diagram 64

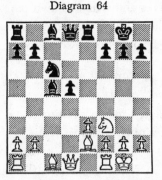

White is clearly on the defensive

---

of opening principles, since White has his hands full trying to catch up in development.

The best chance for White is 11 B—Q 2 and 12 B—B 3.

11.   ... ...   Q—Kt 3!

Black develops his Queen with gain of time by attacking White's unprotected Bishop. White solves the problem by getting rid of the menaced Bishop.

12.   B × Kt   ... ...

White has exchanged the Bishop (which moved three times) for the Knight (which moved only once). Clearly White has lost considerable time. In addition, Black is left with the Bishop-pair against Bishop and Knight, an even more important advantage for Black. From this point on, Black's attacking prospects develop with savage rapidity.

12.   ... ...   P × B

Still another advantage for Black: by recapturing with

the Pawn, he gives the Queen Pawn support. This Pawn is no longer isolated, and thus the last remaining weakness in Black's camp has been removed.

13.   P—Q Kt 3   ... ...

It is indeed high time for White to be thinking of developing his remaining Bishop.

If White tries 13 P—K R 3 (to prevent the irritating pin by ... B—K Kt 5), then Black still maintains a splendid game by 13 ... B—R 3, clearly setting off the impressive power of his two Bishops.

In any event, 13 P—K R 3 is open to the serious objection that it creates a weakness in White's castled position. As the game actually goes, this weakness arises just the same, with consequences that prove fatal for White.

13.   ... ...   **B—K Kt 5!**

The pin on White's Knight sets off Black's advantage in a psychological sense as well as in a technical one.

Diagram 65

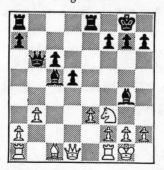

Black has a powerful initiative

The pin confronts White with a baffling problem. His Knight is immobilized because of the pin. His Queen is likewise limited in her movements, because such moves as Q—B 2 or Q—Q 3 permit B × Kt with a resultant break-up of White's Pawns in the castled position. White cannot afford such a break-up, as his King would become too exposed in consequence.

The situation is one which is bound to become intolerable for White. Sooner or later his endurance will snap, and he will try to find some way to free himself from the grip which becomes ever tighter.

14.   B—Kt 2   ... ...

At last this Bishop is developed—an excellent development in itself, but unfortunately it is no contribution to White's pressing problem of finding some effective way of reacting to Black's troublesome pin.

14.   ... ...   **R—K 3!**

Diagram 66

The attack makes progress

With Black's last move, his attack begins to assume really threatening proportions. He intends to maneuver

the Rook into action against White's castled position, ...
R—Kt 3 or ... R—R 3 being promising possibilities.

The alarming aspect of such an attack is that it brings
a force to bear against the castled position which cannot
be parried by a White unit of similar value. So long as
White cannot preserve an equilibrium of defensive force
and offensive force, it is all too likely that the attack
will carry the day.

Generally speaking, it is this local superiority which
makes brilliant sacrifices possible. To sacrifice a piece
when material is even, seems quite a feat. To sacrifice
a piece when you have local superiority and still have
ample material force at the point of attack to compel
your opponent's downfall, appears much less surprising.
And yet no amount of rationalizing and sober theorizing
can quite strip the glamor from a brilliant sacrifice. We
shall have more to say about this later on in the game.

| 15. | R—B 1 | ... ... |

There is little that White can do in the face of Black's
coming attack. The text move, played to keep Black's
King Bishop under attack or to play R—B 2 under some
circumstances, is certainly no worse than anything else
that White might devise.

| 15. | ... ... | R—Kt 3 |

The Rook has been wheeled into action, forcing White
to reckon with the ugly pin ... B—K R 6 at some future
stage.

| 16. | K—R 1 | ... ... |

White eliminates the possibility of falling victim to a
new pin by moving his King and thus making ... B—K

R 6 impossible. This is, however, by no means the end of his troubles.

16.   ... ...   B—Q 3!

Note the steady drift of Black's pieces toward the King-side. Black's Bishop was well placed at Q B 4 but it was not contributing to the direct attack on White's castled King. The Bishop is therefore shifted to the Q 3 square, and from this post it can aim at White's King. Both Black Bishops and his Rook are now involved in the attack, while only White's Knight is offering any defensive resistance to the onslaught.

17.   P—K R 3   ... ...

The concentration of power against his King is getting to be more than White can endure without becoming panicky. Unfortunately for him, the move of the King Rook Pawn is just the kind of weakening that Black requires in order to conclude his attack successfully.

(However, White should not be criticized for weakening his position with the Pawn advance. That advance would have been forced in any event after ... Q—B 2.)

Diagram 67

Black has the desired target

17.   ... ...   Q—B 2!

Now the Queen, the most powerful piece of all, joins the attack. White's Queen has no contribution to make to the defense, so there is now an overwhelming preponderance of attacking units lined up against White's unhappy King.

The immediate problem is: can Black's attacked Bishop be captured? After 18 P × B there follows 18 ... R—R 3 ch; 19 K—Kt 1, B—R 7 ch; and White dare not capture the Bishop because of mate on the move. So 20 K—R 1 is forced, but then 20 ... B—K 4 dis ch; 21 K—Kt 1, B × B; leaves Black with a very superior game. Yet, risky and unattractive as this line of play is for White, it is better than what he gets in the following play.

18.   R—K 1   ... ...

White has calculated through the line of play just shown, and plays his Rook to the K 1 square so as to be able to move his King to K B 1 when the time comes, thus avoiding the discovered check. All very clever, but he fails to see the diabolical resource which Black has available for strengthening the attack.

18.   ... ...   Q—Q 2!!

Now Black extracts the full punishment for the weakening of White's castled position occasioned by the advance of the King Rook Pawn.

(*See Diagram 68*)

Black's threat is 19 ... B × P; 20 P × B, Q × P ch; and mate next move. This is a perfect example of the way in which the advance of a Pawn in front of the castled

Diagram 68

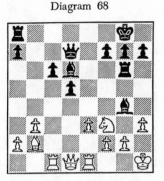

White's castled position is vulnerable

King can result in a compromised position, given a favorable disposition of the enemy's forces.

19.   P × B   ... ...

A dying man can eat anything.

19.   ... ...   **Q × P**

Threatening 20 ... Q × P mate.

If White tries 20 K R—Kt 1, Black forces mate with 20 ... Q—R 4 ch or 20 ... R—R 3 ch.

20.   P—Kt 3   ... ...

Still another weakening Pawn move. But there was no longer any good move. If, for example, 20 Kt—R 4, Q × Kt ch; 21 K—Kt 1, Q—R 7 ch; 22 K—B 1, R × P; 23 Q—Q 2, Q—Kt 8 ch; winning White's Queen. No better is 23 R—B 2 in this variation, for then 23 ... B—Kt 5! is quite decisive.

(See Diagram 69)

20.   ... ...   **Q—R 6 ch**

Diagram 69

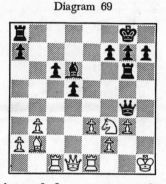

White's castled position is a shambles

If now 21 Kt—R 2, R—R 3; 22 K—Kt 1, B × P!; 23 P × B, Q × P ch; 24 K—B 1, R × Kt; 25 R—B 2.

White seems to have set up a satisfactory position, for the time being, at any rate. Yet Black, a piece down, can come out ahead in material because of the concentrated power of his co-operating Queen and Rook. This is how: 25 ... Q—R 6 ch; 26 K—Kt 1, R—R 8 ch; 27 K—B 2, Q—R 7 ch!; 28 K—B 3, R × R! Now, no matter how Black plays, he is left the Exchange and three Pawns down—a hopeless material minus.

21. K—Kt 1   B × P!
Resigns

White is helpless in the face of this final demolition of his castled position. If 22 P × B, Q × P ch; and Black mates next move. Note that right to the very end, the hard-pressed White King receives no help from the major part of his forces. In such cases, the success of the attack is a foregone conclusion.

SUMMARY: White made one inexact move after another

in the opening, gradually worsening his own position and improving his opponent's. The result was that his pieces could not co-operate for any planned objective, while Black's forces were inexorably brought into action against White's castled position. The result of this cumulative pressure was that White was finally forced to weaken his castled position by making a compromising Pawn move. Thereupon Black took advantage of the situation and, by means of two brilliant Bishop sacrifices, he stripped the castled position of all protecting Pawns and overwhelmed the White King. The relation between White's early transgressions and his later difficulties was very clearly established.

XI

Seize the Initiative with Black Where Possible

CHESS maxims, like popular proverbs, are generalized, superficial rules based on unstated assumptions. To derive any value from them, you must go beyond their immediate directives and search for the hidden premise.

Thus, the apparent wisdom of "Look before you leap" is just as impressive as "He who hesitates is lost." It is equally bewildering to contrast "Opportunity knocks but once" with "Haste makes waste." It is all a question of the specific circumstances, and so we come to the conclusion that the application of proverbs merely follows individual temperament: every man applies that proverb which happens to fit his character.

Chess maxims encounter pretty much the same fate. "Do not try to seize the initiative with the Black pieces" has to be extended: ". . . unless your opponent has played very badly"—or ". . . unless such a policy is fully justified by immensely superior development." The title of this chapter, then, takes on its proper significance only in the context of supposing that inferior play by White makes it possible and justifiable for Black to seize the initiative.

Before we go on to study the very fine game which illustrates this point, it is worth noticing that chess textbooks often puzzle their readers by juxtaposing self-contradictory maxims. Readers save themselves a great deal of confusion by realizing that the apparent contradiction is at once cleared up if the prior assumptions are worked out in every case.

To a certain type of mind, it is a great pity that chess is not an exact science. (If it were, we should not have these contradictions!) But precisely because chess is not an exact science, there is room for imagination, for daring, for plunging into the unknown, for tempting fate, for ever learning new possibilities, new techniques, new sources of enjoying the game.

NIMZO-INDIAN DEFENSE

White	Black
1. P—Q 4	Kt—K B 3

This is the first game which has not started with a Pawn move for both players. The Knight move comes as a shock, because we are accustomed to center Pawn moves at the beginning of the game, in order to begin the fight for control of the center.

However, despite our surprise, we note that 1 ... Kt—K B 3 serves the same purpose as 1 ... P—Q 4: the Knight move, like the Pawn move, prevents White from monopolizing the center by playing 2 P—K 4. And, as 1 ... Kt—K B 3 is a developing move, it seems to have solid qualities despite its flighty appearance.

2. P—Q B 4   ... ...

White means to play P—K 4. Before he begins to fight
for that objective, he first plays the text move to neutralize
Black's possible ... P—Q 4. Thus we have here a very in-
tense fight for control of the center.

2. ... ...   P—K 3

This makes possible the development of Black's King
Bishop, with an objective which becomes clear on the
following move.

3. Kt—Q B 3   ... ...

Now White comes out in the open: he is on the point
of playing P—K 4, with a powerful Pawn center. How
is Black to hold his own in the center?

For one thing, he can play 3 ... P—Q 4; reaching a
Queen's Gambit Declined position by inversion of moves.
But this is too orthodox, perhaps too colorless, for Black.
He prefers a more complicated way of preventing White
from dominating the center area.

3. ... ...   B—Kt 5

An extraordinarily profound move. By pinning White's
Knight, Black prevents White from playing P—K 4. (If
4 P—K 4?, Kt × P; and White cannot recapture.)

(See Diagram 70)

Naturally White does not mean to drop the fight for
control of the center. There are many ways in which
this struggle can be waged, and the method he selects is.
one of the most interesting.

4. Q—B 2   ... ...

Diagram 70

The fight for center control!

Again White supports the contemplated advance of his King Pawn.

    4. ... ...   **Kt—B 3**

Black develops with counterattack. By attacking White's Queen Pawn, he gains time for furthering his own plans, which consist now in allowing White to build up a center with P—K 4, and establishing a counterpoise in the center with ... P—Q 3 and ... P—K 4. As we shall see, this is sound reasoning on Black's part.

    5. Kt—B 3   **... ... ...**

White protects his Queen Pawn with a useful developing move.

    5. ... ...   **P—Q 3**

Black goes ahead with his plan to advance ... P—K 4. Once he has played this move, he has solved the pressing problem of controlling his fair share of the center.

Diagram 71

A crucial decision for White

White is still obsessed with the idea of establishing a broad Pawn center with P—K 4. The effectiveness of this procedure seems somewhat questionable, as Black is prepared to establish himself just as firmly with ... P—K 4. Therefore it seems advisable for White to seek an alternative plan which may be less obviously attractive and yet have more lasting effect.

A good plan, for example, is 6 P—Q R 3, B × Kt ch; 7 Q × B, whereby White obtains the Bishop-pair against Bishop and Knight. In that case, Black will have to observe due precautions against being overwhelmed by the power of the united and co-operating Bishops.

As played, Black has good prospects of counterplay.

6.   B—Kt 5   ... ...

A logical developing move, though not the best. Just as Black pinned White's Queen Knight on the 3rd move to paralyze that Knight's effect on the center, White now pins Black's King Knight to paralyze *that* Knight's effect on the center. But Black is well equipped for taking countermeasures.

6.   ... ...   Castles

Considering castling as a developing move, we find
that each player has made four developing moves. No
better proof is needed to convince us that the defense is
a good one.

Diagram 72

Discretion is the better part of valor

With a little foresight on White's part, he should realize that the seemingly modest 7 P—K 3 is an excellent
move here. The idea is that if 7 ... P—K 4; 8 P—Q 5
drives back Black's Queen Knight, as ... Kt—Q 5 is impossible.

This is a point worthy of careful note. The average
player is rarely sensitive to the effectiveness of judicious
Pawn moves in limiting the mobility of hostile Knights.
This technique is part of the stock-in-trade of every master, and it helps to explain why the Knight is often inferior
to the Bishop.

7.   P—K 4   P—K 4

Black fights for the center. If now 8 P × P, P × P; and
Black still has ... Kt—Q 5 in reserve.

8. P—Q 5   ... ...

This aggressive advance can still yield White a good
game if followed up properly.

8. ... ...   Kt—Q 5

An aggressive counterthrust, so aggressive, in fact, that
White fails to find the best reply.

What makes this move look so formidable is that one's
first impression is that after 9 Kt × Kt, P × Kt; White
must lose his pinned Knight. However, this impression is
deceptive. The power of the pin is great indeed, as we
have often seen in earlier games. But here White is fortunate enough to have excellent counterplay.

Diagram 73

How should White meet the threat?

White's proper course is 9 Kt × Kt!, P × Kt; and now
counterattack on the pinning Bishop: 10 P—Q R 3! After
10 ... B × Kt ch; 11 P × B, P × P; 12 B—Q 3!, White
has a satisfactory game, in view of his Bishop-pair and
the continuation of his pin on Black's Knight. He is temporarily a Pawn down; but this Pawn is unsupported and
can be picked up later on.

By playing the recommended move 9 Kt × Kt!, White gets on with his development and maintains his Bishops at their most effective functioning level.

9.   Q—Q 3   ... ...

Instead, White "plays it safe," which in this case happens to be a course fraught with danger!

9.   ... ...   P—K R 3

Diagram 74

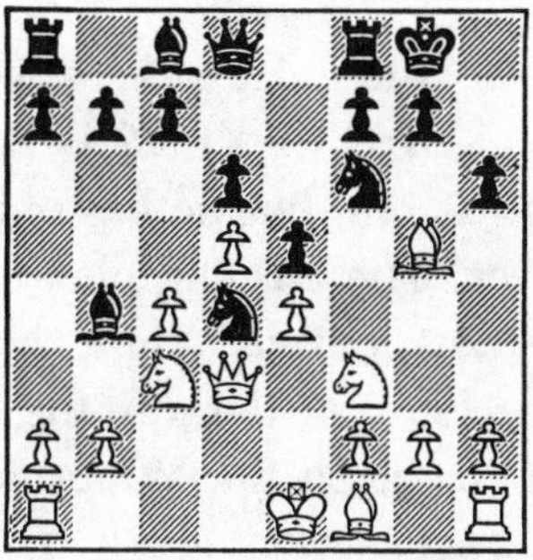

Another crucial decision for White

How shall White dispose of the attacked Bishop? To play 10 B × Kt leaves Black with the Bishop-pair and a well-entrenched Knight at his Q 5 square. This line involves still another source of discomfort for White: he would be left with his King Bishop, a piece whose mobility is seriously hampered by the White Pawns on white squares.

White concludes that he ought to retain his "black-square" Bishop. A sound conclusion, but where should the Bishop be played? The right move is 10 B—Q 2!, releasing Black's pin and also "putting the question" to

Black's entrenched Knight. Most important of all, perhaps, is the point that after 10 B—Q 2!, the Bishop still has access to the center squares, with a potentially valuable future ahead of him.

10.   B—R 4?   ... ...

This obsession with the pin turns out disastrously for White. As in the play on page 64, the Bishop is "decentralized" and driven into exile.

10.   ... ...   **P—K Kt 4!**

A courageous decision! He does not fear the typical sacrifice 11 Kt × Kt P, P × Kt; 12 B × P. In that event White maintains the pin, but he has only two Pawns for the sacrificed piece. The ensuing play requires great patience on Black's part; but, as White has no resources for reinforcing the pressure of the pin, the sacrifice must be considered inadequate. So the White Bishop retreats to his melancholy refuge.

11.   B—Kt 3   ... ...

The Bishop will now remain out of play for the remainder of the game.

11.   ... ...   **Kt × K P!!**

(*See Diagram 75*)

Profiting by White's earlier inexactitudes, Black seizes the initiative with a brilliant surprise move.

The point is that if 12 Q × Kt??, B—K B 4!; 13 Q—K 3, Kt—B 7 ch; and Black forks King and Queen.

12.   K Kt × Kt   ... ...

Diagram 75

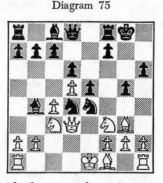

Black seizes the initiative

White wants to maintain material equality, but from now on he is harried unceasingly by Black's energetic attacking measures.

12.	P × Kt
13. Q × P	... ...

And not 13 Q × Kt??, R—K 1; when Black pins—and wins—White's Queen. The sacrifice has had the explosive effect of bringing all of Black's pieces to life with irresistible power.

13.	R—K 1

Getting the Rook into play with no loss of time. The immediate threat is 13 ... Kt × B dis ch or 13 ... Kt × Kt dis ch with catastrophe for White.

Note that for the balance of the play, there is no opportunity for White to take advantage of the advance of Black's Pawns in front of his castled King. Under ordinary circumstances, this advance would have been seriously compromising. But here the circumstances are not ordinary: White has neither the development, nor the time, to embark on any counterattack.

Diagram 76

White must parry the threat on the King file

White would like to castle on the King-side, but this is hardly feasible: for example 14 B—K 2, B—K B 4. Now if 15 Castles K R?, there follows 15 ... Kt × B.

To reply 16 B P × Kt?? is disastrous, as it allows the pin 16 ... B—B 4 winning White's Queen.

Hence White must continue 16 R P × Kt, but then 16 ... B × Kt; wins a piece because White's remaining Bishop at his K 2 square is attacked.

So Black decides to castle on the Queen-side; but here too life is no bed of roses!

14. Castles   Kt × Kt

Observe that 14 ... Kt × B is much weaker, as it opens the King Rook file for White with counterattacking possibilities.

Another virtue of the exchange in the text is that it breaks up the Pawn position in front of White's castled

King. The resulting Pawn configuration is such that White's King is somewhat isolated from the rest of his forces.

15.   P × Kt   B—R 6 ch

Black gains time with one move after the other: each move is made with a threat.

Diagram 77

White's King is on the run

It would be pleasant for White to be able to tuck his King safely away in the corner, but that turns out to be impossible. For if 16 K—Kt 1?, B—B 4 ch!; and now 17 B—Q 3?? will not do because of 17 ... B—B 4! trapping the White Queen. (There are some pretty instances hereabouts of the attacking power of two menacing Bishops.)

But 16 K—Kt 1?, B—B 4 ch!; 17 K—R 1 will not do either, because of 17 ... B—B 7; when White must lose the Exchange: if 18 R—Q 2?, R—K 8 ch; ends it all.

16.   K—B 2   B—B 4 ch

Here again it is fatal to interpose 17 B—Q 3??, because of 17 ... B—B 4!; trapping White's Queen.

17.   K—Kt 3   ... ...

Now Black must do something about his Bishop at Q R 6 which is under attack. His solution of the problem is electrifying.

Diagram 78

Another brilliant attacking move

17.   ... ...   **P—B 4!!**

Superb play. If White captures the Pawn in passing,* there follows 17 ... B—B 4!; 18 Q—Q 2, Q—Kt 3 ch; 19 K—R 4, Q—R 3 ch; 20 K—Kt 3, Q—R 6 mate!

18.   Q—Q 2   **Q—R 4**

Black is now ready for the final phase of the attack.

19.   B—Q 3   ... ...

White hopefully develops the Bishop at last, but this comes much too late!

---

* For the benefit of readers who may be hazy about capturing in passing, the effect is as if Black had played ... P—Q B 3 and White had replied P × P.

He is philosophically prepared for 19 ... B—Q 2 (threatens mate); 20 K—B 2, B—R 5 ch; winning the exchange for Black.

Instead, Black has a stunning reply which quickly decides in his favor.

Diagram 79

The decisive attack begins

    19. ... ...   **P—Kt 4!!**

Threatens 20 ... Q—R 5 mate!

Flight by means of 20 K—B 2 is unavailing: 20 ... Q—R 5 ch; 21 K—Kt 1, B × B ch; 22 Q × B, P × P; 23 Q—Q 2, Q R—Kt 1 ch; 24 K—R 1, B—Kt 7 ch; 25 Q × B, R × Q; 26 K × R, R—K 7 ch; forcing checkmate.

    20. P × P   ... ...

This move also allows an elegant breakthrough. The sustained dynamic character of Black's play is truly remarkable.

    20. ... ...   **B × B**

Preparing for another Pawn sacrifice.

    21. Q × B   **P—B 5 ch!!**

An exquisite move which forces the opening of the Queen Bishop file for Black's offensive.

22. Q × P   ... ...

Or 22 K × P, Q—R 5 mate! Black conducts the whole game with rare imaginative verve.

22. ... ...   **Q R—B 1**

One must admire the adroit way in which Black has made the Queen Bishop file available for his attack.

23. Q—Q 3   ... ...

The only choice left to White is to select the manner of his loss. Thus, if 23 Q—Q R 4, Black has two ways to mate on the move.

Or if 23 Q—Q 4, R—K 5!; 24 Q—Q 3, Q—R 5 mate!

23. ... ...   **R—K 5!**

Diagram 80

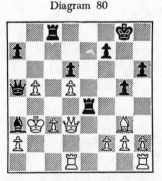

The final brilliant sacrifice

As in the previous game, we see how overwhelming local superiority makes it possible for the aggressor to indulge in the most spectacular sacrifices.

If now 24 Q × R, R × P mate.

Meanwhile Black threatens 24 ... Q—R 5 mate.

| 24. | K—B 2 | R/K 5—Q B 5 |

Resigns

There was no longer any defense to Black's massive push against the Queen Bishop Pawn.

If, for example, 25 K—Kt 1, Q × P ch; and mate next move.

And if 25 K—Q 2, R × P; with a crushing discovered check which at the very least wins White's Queen.

SUMMARY: As in the previous game, slight errors of judgment on White's part permitted Black to seize the initiative. As Black's offensive progressed, the tempo of the attack increased and White's King was battered by the assault of Black's pieces until the defense became untenable.

PART II

Problems of Strategy

XII

How to Maneuver with the
Two Bishops

To USE the two Bishops for direct attack against the King
is relatively easy. The target is clearly indicated, the goal
is known. To maneuver with the two Bishops where
direct attack is out of the question, is much more difficult. For this type of play belongs to the department of
positional chess, which calls for foresight and patience.

What is our guiding thought in maneuvering with the
two Bishops? Our goal here is to increase our command
of the board. The two Bishops are greedy. They start
with a certain amount of superior mobility. If the situation favors us, we must increase that margin of superior
mobility. We must gradually force the opponent to give
way, to allow the Bishops to obtain more and more mobility.

As the Bishops gain ground, the opponent's command
of the board shrinks and shrivels. He begins to find his
choice of moves more and more limited. If he plays a
certain move, he finds that he allows a further infiltra-

tion into his position. If he tries a different move, the infiltration occurs in another form. And so it goes. The
Bishops advance from success to success, and each time
the opponent finds his course of action becoming more
and more limited.

To handle the Bishops in this way requires real skill,
a skill that necessitates considerable training and practice. But the first step is to become *aware* of the power
of the Bishops.

We have already touched in one or two games on the
technique of limiting the opposing Knight's moves by
judicious Pawn moves. This is of the greatest importance
in the play with the two Bishops. By making the appropriate Pawn moves, we cut down the Knight's mobility.
This in turn enhances the power of our Bishops, and the
co-operation of our Bishops and our Pawns is a valuable
factor in achieving the goal of reducing the opponent to
"movelessness."

Ruy Lopez

White	Black
1. P—K 4	P—K 4
2. Kt—K B 3	Kt—Q B 3
3. B—Kt 5	P—Q R 3

These moves are already familiar to us from earlier
games. The usual reply at this point is 4 B—R 4.

4. B × Kt	... ...

This early exchange gives Black two Bishops against
Bishop and Knight. If White hopes for any countervail-
ing advantage, it does not become apparent during the
course of this game.

4. ... ...   **Q P × B**

As we know, White cannot win a Pawn now by 5
Kt × P, as Black recovers his Pawn by 5 ... Q—Kt 4 or
5 ... Q—Q 5.

5. P—K R 3   **... ... ...**

This is rather questionable. White need not fear the
pin by ... B—K Kt 5 unduly in this position, as Black
lacks the possibility of ... Kt—Q 5, his Queen Knight
having been exchanged. (See page 64 on this point.)
The pin, if allowed, is therefore not too painful.

As played, White has lost a move and laid the ground-
work for a possible shift of the initiative to Black. This
may lead to a really critical situation for White, as he is
still in need of some asset in his position to balance
Black's advantage of the Bishop-pair. It is true that in
this rather characterless position, that advantage is still
in a nebulous state.

5. ... ...   **Kt—B 3**

In contrast to his opponent, Black develops.

6. P—Q 3   **B—Q 3**

Interestingly enough, Black is actually ahead in development, the consequence of White's loss of time at his
5th move.

7. Kt—B 3   **Castles**
8. Castles   **... ... ...**

Both players are proceeding with their development.

8. ... ...   **P—Q Kt 3**

A questionable move. Black intends to play ... B—Kt 2 followed by ... P—B 4. This gives the Queen Bishop a diagonal of sorts, but it is trained on White's King Pawn, which is securely guarded by his Queen Pawn.

Diagram 81

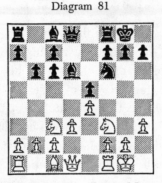

Black's Bishops can be held in check

White is fortunate in having a position which offers little scope to the Black Bishops. Black's King Bishop is blocked by his King Pawn, and therefore has minimal scope. The other Black Bishop, as we have seen, is not destined to be very effective. We conclude that it is clearly in White's interest to keep the position closed. In this way the influence of the Bishops is very mild indeed.

With the Pawn position in the center stabilized and immobile, White should devise a plan which will avoid any increase of scope for the Bishops. A good plan is 9 Kt—R 2 with a view to 10 P—B 4. This opens the King Bishop file for White's King Rook, giving White offensive possibilities on the King-side without renouncing the stabilized situation in the center.

9. P—Q 4?   ... ...

But this is faulty strategy. The center is now in a fluid state, the position is opened up, the Bishops come to life, and the short-stepping Knights find themselves at a disadvantage. This observation gives us some notion of the faulty character of White's last move; but it will require the actual unfolding of the play to appreciate to the full how White has compromised his chances.

9. ... ...   **P × P**

The first consequence for Black is that his King Pawn, which blocked the action of the King Bishop, has disappeared. At once the effectiveness of this Bishop is greatly enhanced.

10. Kt × P   **B—Kt 2**

The other Bishop also becomes active. Now that the center is fluid, the solid protection of White's King Pawn is no longer available. This Pawn is vulnerable to attack, Black's immediate threat being 11 ... P—B 4, attacking White's Knight at his Q 4 square and thereby winning his King Pawn.

Diagram 82

Black's Bishops have come to life

Thus one move (9 P—Q 4?) was enough to change the character of the position from a close one to an open one, with a vast increase in the Bishop's mobility, and a corresponding decrease in the powers of White's Knights.

11.   R—K 1   ... ...

This gives the King Pawn the needed protection; but White is already on the defensive.

11.   ... ...   B—K 4!

Having been given his opportunity, Black does not relax the pressure. Operating with the direct threat of winning a piece by ... B × Kt, Black *centralizes* this Bishop more powerfully. Note how this bears out the introductory comment on the Bishop's greed for more and more terrain. Note, also, that the excellent text move has been made possible by the disappearance of Black's King Pawn.

12.   K Kt—K 2   ... ...

This retreat is distasteful, as it is a step in the direction of submitting to the Knight's gradual loss of mobility. Yet the alternative 12 B—K 3 will not do because of 12 ... P—B 4, winning the King Pawn. This illustrates the introductory comment on the technique of combining Bishop moves and Pawn moves for the purpose of constricting the Knights.

12.   ... ...   Q × Q

Black readily exchanges Queens, for it is in the end-game that the Bishops most easily demonstrate their superiority. The reason for this is that the Queen, being by far the most powerful piece, can often organize diversions which deflect the game from its indicated logical course. But the simplifying exchange technique rules out such diversionary possibilities.

13.   R × Q   ... ...

Ordinarily, White's occupation of the open file would be distinctly in his favor. Here this occupation is of little importance, as it is overshadowed by Black's potent two-Bishop pressure. Actually it will be Black who will seize the open file, while White is preoccupied with the problem of resisting the encroachment of the Bishops.

And this suggests to us still another powerful argument in favor of the Bishops. While the opponent is busy resisting their aggressions, he is often compelled to concede some other point: he cannot fight all along the line.

On the other hand, we must not lose sight of the fact that the exploitation of the Bishops is not a soulless, mechanical process. It requires forethought and precaution. Without these qualities, we may allow an alert opponent to escape from the pressure, or at all events greatly increase his powers of resistance. In this position, for example, White is on the point of improving his prospects with P—B 4 followed by P—K 5. This would by no means neutralize the advantage of the Bishops, but it would leave White with a much less constricted position than he has in the text continuation.

13.   ... ...   P—B 4!

Again menacing the King Pawn, and thereby compelling White to resort to a timid defensive move.

14.   P—B 3   ... ...

This defends the King Pawn securely, but at the cost of giving White a far less aggressive position than he would have if P—B 4 were possible.

14.   ... ...   **Q R—Q 1**

Black fights for the open file.

15.   B—Kt 5   ... ...

Pinning the Knight and threatening to free himself with 16 P—B 4, when Black can hardly avoid parting with his King Bishop.

15.   ... ...   **P—Kt 4!**

Another good move to restrain and drive back the White Knights.

Diagram 83

White's Knights are forced back

White finds that he can play 16 P—B 4 only at the cost of a Pawn: 16 ... R × R ch; 17 Kt × R, Kt × P! Or 17 R × R, B × Kt; 18 Kt × B, Kt × P; etc.

Meanwhile Black is threatening 16 ... B—B 3; followed

by ... P—Kt 5. The Knights are proving more and more unequal to the situation, and White resigns himself to passive defense.

16.	Q R—Kt 1	R × R ch
17.	R × R	... ...

Now White has the open file again, but profits precious little from it.

17.	... ...	B—B 3!

A fine move. He prevents Kt—R 4 in reply to the coming ... P—Kt 5. In addition, he prevents a possible R—Q 7 in the event that the Black Knight should leave his present square.

Meanwhile White must find something against the coming ... P—Kt 5, which threatens to win White's Queen Knight Pawn.

18.	P—R 3?	... ...

He could put up a better fight with 18 P—Q Kt 3.

18.	... ...	P—Kt 5
19.	P × P	P × P
20.	Kt—R 2	B—Kt 4!

(See Diagram 84)

From move to move the Bishops have been becoming more powerful. Just as ominous for White is the fact that the Black Queen-side Pawns are advancing steadily. As Black has three Pawns to two on that wing, the advance should result eventually in a powerful passed Pawn, strongly supported by the Bishops. (Note how the advancing Pawns aid the Bishops in reducing the mobility

Diagram 84

The Bishops increase their power

---

of the Knights; while the Bishops in turn support the advancing Pawns. An ideal example of co-operation!)

As for White, his four Pawns to three on the King-side do not have the same likelihood of being transformed into a passed Pawn. This is due in large part to the enforced defensive formation of White Pawns on his K 4 square and K B 3 square. As long as White has to maintain this lifeless formation, his prospects of counterplay are meager indeed.

21.	**K—B 2**	... ...

White protects the attacked Knight, and at the same time begins bringing his King to the center to aid in the defense.

21.	... ...	**P—B 4**

Black protects his Queen Knight Pawn in order to threaten ... B × P himself.

22.	**P—Q Kt 3**	**P—Q R 4**

White has no good counter, in the long run, to the advance of these Pawns.

23. K—K 3   ... ...

White still hopes that with due preparation he will be able to play P—K B 4.

23. ... ...   **P—R 3!**

This sets White a very difficult problem.

Diagram 85

Where should White's Bishop play?

The attacked Bishop has three possible moves, of which 24 B—B 4?? is quite out of the question, as 24 ... B × Kt wins a piece for Black.

Relatively best seems 24 B × Kt, B × B; 25 R—Q 6, giving White some counterplay, at this late date, against Black's Queen-side Pawns. However, White is understandably reluctant to part with his remaining Bishop. As a rule, two Knights are quite helpless against two Bishops.

24. B—R 4   ... ...

White retains the Bishop, but Black is able to make considerable further headway just the same.

> 24. ... ...   **P—Kt 4!**

With this and his next move—both of them excellent —Black establishes such a "bind" on the King-side that White's Pawns on that wing can never be mobilized.

> 25. **B—K 1**   **B × Kt!**

Black plays with remarkably fine judgment. He gives up one of the precious Bishops in order to be able to operate more effectively with the other. This is a typical transaction for the player who has the Bishop-pair: whenever a favorable opportunity offers, he can give up one of the Bishops, transforming his advantage into some other type of advantage.

Note, by the way, that Black holds on to the right Bishop. His remaining Bishop still remains strongly centralized, and what is just as important, the Bishop aims at White's Queen-side—the area in which the decisive march forward of his Queen-side Pawns must take place.

> 26. **K × B**   ... ...

Now Black should play 26 ... P—R 5!; when victory is within his grasp. If then 27 P × P, R—R 1; with a winning position. And if White does not play 27 P × P, Black still continues ... R—R 1 with a winning game.

> 26. ... ...   **B—Q 5?**
> 27. **P—B 3?**   ... ...

This is a double mistake.

In the first place, by playing 27 B—B 2, White can

force the exchange of Bishops, whereupon the Black Queen-side Pawns, hitherto so formidable but now deprived of support, may suddenly turn out to be weak.

Secondly, White's Pawn move is a mistake because, as we know, Pawn captures, or the possibility of Pawn captures, makes line-opening possible. And the opening of lines on the Queen-side can only benefit the aggressor—in this case, Black.

| 27. ... ... | B—K 4! |

Black has recovered the thread of the game again. Apparently White artlessly expected 27 ... P × P?; 28 B × P, when the Queen-side Pawns are stopped, and exposed to attack as well.

After the text move, Black threatens 28 ... P—B 5!; 29 Kt P × P, P—Kt 6; 30 Kt—B 1, P—R 5; and the two powerful passed Pawns must win the game for Black.

| 28. P × P | ... ... |

Likewise after 28 P—Q B 4, Black has a winning position, 28 ... P—R 5!; being indicated.

| 28. ... ... | R P × P! |

Again we have an example of the usefulness of Pawn captures to the aggressor. White can devise nothing to hold the game in the face of the coming ... R—R 1.

| 29. R—B 1 | ... ... |

At this late date, White wants to stamp the Queen Bishop Pawn as a weakness. But Black is fully prepared to break through.

Diagram 86

Black forces a winning passed Pawn

Now Black must win, and, logically enough, by seizing the open Queen Rook file.

29. ... ...   R—R 1!

To this there is only one reply:

30. R—B 2   P—B 5!!

This wins in all variations, the main point being, of course, that if 31 R × P?, R × Kt ch; wins a piece.

The alternative 31 P × P? allows the crushing Pawn fork 31 ... P—Kt 6; and White can resign. The same effect is achieved by 31 B × P?, P × P; etc.

31. Kt × P   P × P

At last Black has the deadly passed Pawn for which he has played so patiently and so ably.

32. R—B 1   P—Kt 7

Supported by the Bishop, this Pawn must carry the day.

33. R—Kt 1   R—R 8
Resigns

For White must give up his Rook to prevent the Pawn from queening.

SUMMARY: White needlessly gave his opponent the advantage of the Bishop-pair against Bishop and Knight. Then, just as needlessly, he opened up the game when he should have kept the center closed in order to minimize the power of the Bishop-pair. From then on, the Bishops steadily gained in power and Black's Queen-side majority of Pawns became ever more menacing. At the right moment, Black parted with the less valuable of his Bishops; but then, well within sight of his goal, he faltered and gave White an opportunity to save himself. But White was blind to the chance offered to him. He thereupon succumbed to the inevitable, in the form of a well-supported Black Pawn which marched down to queen.

XIII

How to Attack Weak Pawns

AFTER studying eleven games in which the hostile King is the noble quarry that is being hunted, it seems quite a comedown to seek such base prey as the Pawn. Yet the change is buttressed by good common sense, and the transition is less abrupt than might be supposed.

The direct attack against the King is no doubt the most interesting feature of chess, and the one most appropriate against a weak opponent, or at least an opponent who happens to be playing a particular game weakly. Yet our opponents are not always weak, nor do they always play weakly, nor would we want them to. In well-contested games the direct attack is often impossible, and we must be content to train our sights on less glaring targets.

The Pawn makes an excellent target *because it cannot retreat*. If it is unfavorably situated, for one reason or another, it must either submit to attack on the unfavorable square, or try to advance. However, as advancing only brings it closer to the enemy's forces, the effect of advancing is as a rule to make the Pawn more vulnerable to hostile pressure.

Sometimes, it is true, a weak Pawn can be exchanged; but, as the option of exchanging generally lies in the aggressor's power, he will take measures to avoid the exchange—or submit to it only by exacting a price in the form of some other advantage. And so the problem of the weak Pawn remains to plague the defender.

One of the evils which a weak Pawn brings in its wake is that its existence compels the defender to assign pieces to guard it. As we know, the value of a Pawn is far less than that of a piece. The consequence—a highly unsatisfactory one—is that pieces must be employed in a highly uneconomical manner to guard units of lesser value.

As a rule, the attacker will benefit by this state of affairs through being able to deploy to good effect those of his own pieces which are not similarly burdened. What usually happens, in that case, is that the defender's pieces cannot function at their most effective level. Sooner or later, the defender must either abandon the Pawn or fall a victim to some other disadvantage. This is almost inevitable when the defender's forces are spread too thin.

We see, then, that the defense of a weak Pawn may have far-reaching effects which are even more serious than the loss of a Pawn. And yet the loss of a Pawn is almost certain to result in a lost ending. Such are the dilemmas which confront the unfortunate player who is burdened with a weak Pawn!

BIRD'S OPENING

White	Black
1. P—K B 4	... ...

It is no accident that this opening move is unusual. We can say categorically that the average player's best course in the opening is to begin by moving a center Pawn—King Pawn or Queen Pawn—and thus at once preparing for a rapid and rational development.

White's first move here has the virtue of controlling the important K 5 square. But 1 P—Q 4 has the same quality, while at the same time facilitating White's quick and natural development. In the hands of an inexperienced player, 1 P—K B 4 may be the first step to perdition in the sense that he may succumb to a thoughtless neglect of development.

1. ... ...   P—Q 4

A good reply. Black takes up the fight for the center squares, and at the same time he does not neglect possibilities of developing his pieces.

2. Kt—K B 3   ... ...

As always, this is a good developing move.

2. ... ...   P—Q B 4

The advance of this Pawn is good policy in the close openings. For one thing, the Pawn commands an important square in the .center: Black's Q 5 square. In addition, Black gives his pieces more playing room—he provides, for example, for his later move ... Q—B 2. Without playing ... P—Q B 4, Black would subsequently lack a good square for his Queen.

3. P—K 3   ... ...

Now White prepares for the development of his King Bishop.

3. ... ...   Kt—K B 3

Black proceeds with the development of his King-side forces.

Diagram 87

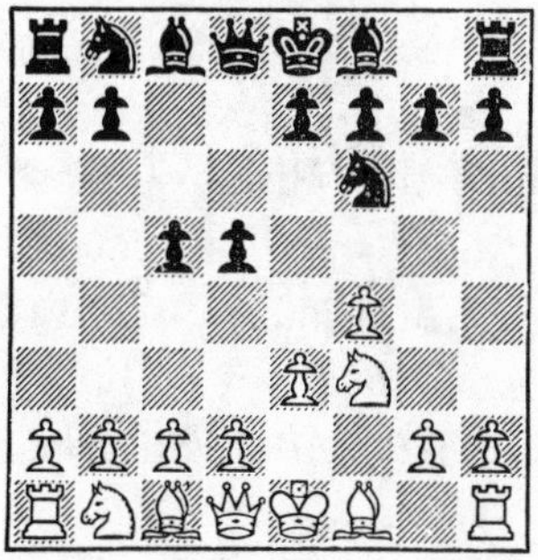

An opening finesse

We have often observed how a lack of foresight in the opening has serious consequences in the later part of the game. Here is a case in point.

White courts trouble by failing to think through the problem of developing his Bishops. It may seem astonishing that this problem should arise as early as the 4th move. But the problem arises here because White has selected an unnatural opening move. We may take it as certain that an unnatural opening move will require an unnatural sequel.

White's basic difficulty is that it is hopeless to think of developing his Queen Bishop along its natural diagonal. The most useful squares have been pre-empted by the moves 1 P—K B 4 and 3 P—K 3. Hence, if the Queen Bishop is to have any future worth thinking about, it must be developed in fianchetto—on Q Kt 2, after the preliminary P—Q Kt 3.

It is true that the Bishop will then have splendid scope

along the long diagonal. But then a new problem arises: is the Queen Pawn to be advanced one square or two? (Note again that all this debate is occasioned by White's unnatural 1 P—K B 4.)

If, after playing his Queen Bishop to Q Kt 2, White advances P—Q 4, he will block his Queen Bishop's proud diagonal and reduce that Bishop almost to the status of a Pawn. Another diagreeable aspect of P—Q 4 is that, coming after P—K B 4, it leaves White's K 4 square without Pawn protection—makes it a "hole." (On this point, see the ninth game, page 104.) So apparently P—Q 4 is ruled out.

Should White, then, consider advancing the Queen Pawn only one square? This seems to make sense, for in that case the diagonal of his Queen Bishop remains clear and open. But in that event, what of White's other Bishop?! Hemmed in by the Pawn at Q 3, the King Bishop will be doomed to futility.

The upshot of all this reflection is that White should play P—Q 3 in due course to leave the fianchettoed Queen Bishop a clear line of action—but that right now his indicated course is 4 B—Kt 5 ch, enabling him to exchange his King Bishop for Black's Queen Bishop (4 B—Kt 5 ch, B—Q 2; 5 B × B ch, etc.) or for Black's Queen Knight (after 4 ... Kt—Q 2 or 4 ... Kt—Q B 3). In this way White would dispose of a problem which is bound to have serious repercussions on his development and on his hopes of later success.

4.   B—K 2?   ... ...

Completely missing the point. As our reasoning about this position has demonstrated, White's proper course is

4 B—Kt 5 ch, ridding himself of a piece which is likely to be a liability rather than an asset.

4.   ... ...   **P—K Kt 3!**

Well played. Black is alive to the potentialities of this position, and he foresees that White can hardly avoid fianchettoing his Queen Bishop. He therefore fianchettoes his own King Bishop as a counterpoise to the pressure which will be exerted by the White Bishop on the diagonal.

5.   P—Q Kt 3   **... ... ...**

White develops the Queen Bishop on the only suitable diagonal.

5.   ... ...   **B—Kt 2**
6.   B—Kt 2   **Castles**

Diagram 88

Black's development is satisfactory

Black can be quite content with his development. He has none of the problems which plague White, and the rest of his pieces will be developed with equal facility.

The only feature of White's development of which he can be proud is his command of the important K 5 square—although this is neutralized to some extent by Black's King Bishop.

Regarding the White and Black Bishops on the long diagonal, it is important to observe that the Black King Bishop is guarded by the Black King and is therefore not subject to tactical surprises; the White Bishop, being unprotected, is theoretically vulnerable to tactical surprises. This point will play a role in the subsequent proceedings.

7. Kt—K 5   ... ...

White is in a hurry to occupy the important square, but his occupancy is of short duration.

7. ... ...   **Q—B 2**

A useful preliminary to ... Kt—B 3. If at once 7 ... Kt—B 3; 8 Kt × Kt, P × Kt; and Black is left with an unwieldy doubled Pawn. Hence the text move, which prepares to undermine White's most aggressively posted piece.

8. Castles   **Kt—B 3**

Here White is confronted with the unpleasant possibility of ... Kt—Q 2 (or even ... Kt—K 1), creating a pin on the advanced Knight because White's Bishop at Q Kt 2 is unprotected. True, White can support the advanced Knight at his K 5 square by P—Q 4; but, as explained earlier, he is understandably reluctant to create a hole at his K 4 square.

9. Kt × Kt   **Q × Kt**

The upshot of White's proud occupation of his K 5 square is that his best-posted piece has disappeared; that Black is already ahead in development; and that White is now confronted with a new difficulty: how to develop his Queen Knight. After Kt—R 3, the Knight has hardly any scope, as is usual when a Knight is played to the edge of the board. After Kt—B 3, the Knight blocks the diagonal of the fianchettoed Bishop. White concludes, therefore, that Kt—Q 2 is the proper development. He prepares for this development with the following move.

10.   P—Q 3?   ... ...

But this move, plausible as it looks, is premature! Correct was first 10 B—KB 3, making room for Q—K 2 as necessary. Naturally Black would have retained a highly satisfactory position in this case as well.

10.   ... ...   **Q—K 3!**

Alertly played, and taking advantage of White's inexactitude.

Diagram 89

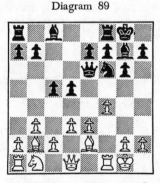

White is embarrassed

It is not easy for White to protect the King Pawn without seriously upsetting his scheme of development. Thus, 11 Q—Q 2 makes it impossible for the Knight to play to Q 2 as contemplated. And of course 11 K—B 2?? would be a ghastly blunder in view of 11 ... Kt—K 5 ch!; 11 P × Kt, B × B followed by ... B × R. (Compare the previous comment on the significance of the unprotected state of White's Queen Bishop.)

However, after 11 K—B 2??, Black accomplishes nothing with 11 ... Kt—Kt 5 ch?; 12 B × Kt!, when Black's Queen is *en prise!*

| 11. | Q—B 1 | ... ... |

Thus White guards the weak King Pawn and the fianchettoed Bishop as well. But such fussy guardian duty is hardly calculated to exploit to the full the magnificent powers of the Queen!

Incidentally, it must not be thought that Black suffers any inconvenience from the placement of his Queen at his K 3 square. As his King Bishop is admirably developed, there is no need for his King Pawn to move; and his Queen Bishop is likewise not hampered, having an excellent square reserved for it at Black's Q Kt 2 square.

| 11. | ... ... | P—Kt 3 |
| 12. | Kt—R 3 | ... ... |

(*See Diagram 90*)

As 12 Kt—Q 2 is not feasible and 12 Kt—B 3 is undesirable, this unnatural and ineffectual "development" of the Knight is practically compulsory. Black's Knight, on the other hand, operates effectively in the vicinity of

Diagram 90

Unsatisfactory development for the White Knight

---

the center squares. Thus White is still suffering from the
effects of his opening move.

12. ... ...   B—Kt 2

Both Black Bishops are admirably trained on the center,
and Black's position in general has a pleasing air of har-
monious co-operation on the part of his pieces. The impression in White's camp is, however, quite different.

13. B—K B 3   ... ...

For the first time in the game, this Bishop is well placed.
White prepares for the pinning move P—B 4, which will
give his pieces more maneuvering space.

13. ... ...   Q R—B 1

This is the only move on Black's part which is open to
criticism. He can save a whole move by playing ... Q R—
Q 1 directly, to be followed by ... R—Q 2 and ... K R—Q 1.
However, his positional advantage is so manifest that he
can afford the luxury of a lost tempo.

14. P—B 4	... ...

White's position is becoming a bit more comfortable in appearance, but the decentralized Knight is still an eyesore, and the weak King Pawn still requires protection.

14.	K R—Q 1

Black shows good judgment in bringing a Rook to this file, which is bound to be opened sooner or later. Any opening of the file will uncover still another weak White Pawn: the Queen Pawn.

15. R—K 1	... ...

At long last, the Rook takes over the protection of the ailing King Pawn, relieving White's Queen of her nursemaid assignment.

15.	R—Q 2

Preparing to double the Rooks, but 15 ... R—B 2 serves the same purpose and is a trifle more accurate.

16. Q—B 2	... ...

Just when the Queen is about to achieve freedom, a new form of slavery appears.

16.	P × P!

A case of perfect timing.

(See Diagram 91)

Black's capture has been admirably timed. For if now 17 B × B, P × Q P!; 18 B × R, P × Q; 19 B × R, Q × B; 20 Kt × P, Q—Q 7; and White is hopelessly tied up. Even in this variation, White's unwieldy development handicaps him bitterly.

Diagram 91

More Pawn weaknesses for White

Alternatives are of little avail in the long run, for example: 17 Q P × P, B × B; 18 P × B, R/B 1—Q 1. Now Black threatens ... R—Q 7 and White cannot oppose Rooks on the Queen file without losing the weak King Pawn. (This is a good example of the way defense of weak Pawns extorts positional concessions.) After 19 R—K 2, Q—R 6! (more pressure on weak Pawns); 20 R—B 2, Kt—Kt 5!!; Black wins; for if 21 P × Kt, B × B; and White cannot play 22 Q × B because of 22 ... R—Q 8 ch forcing mate. A remarkable example of positional pressure reinforced by tactical threats to a point beyond the defender's endurance!

17.   Kt P × P   ... ...

White has avoided the deadly infiltration on the Queen file, but the move actually played leaves him with more Pawn weaknesses than he can possibly defend.

17.	... ...	**B × B**
18.	**P × B**	**R/B 1—Q 1**

Black can concentrate on no less than four weak White Pawns! The Queen Pawn is the most obvious target, as it can be attacked by Black's Queen and Rooks.

19.   Q R—Q 1   ... ...

White defends as best he can, although passive defense has been his lot since the opening branched off into the middle game.

19.   ... ...   Q—B 4!

Diagram 92

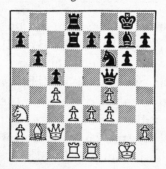

Black strengthens the pressure

Black's Queen move, attacking the Queen Pawn for the third time, forces White's reply, as 20 P—K 4 loses a Pawn at once.

20.   P—Q 4   Q × Q

Heading right for the endgame, as he sees that he must soon win a Pawn.

21.   Kt × Q   ... ...

The weak Pawns have gained a new defender, but material loss is unavoidable all the same.

21. ... ...   Kt—R 4!

Diagram 93

White must lose a Pawn

The weakness of the Pawn at White's Q 4 square is now linked with that of the Pawn at his K B 4 square. (When the Queen Pawn has an earache, the King Bishop Pawn has a toothache.)

As White's crowning misfortune, his Queen Pawn is pinned two ways—on the Queen file and on the long diagonal. (Thus Black has won the duel of the Bishops on the long diagonal!)

22. K—B 2   P—K 3

Black is in no hurry to win the Pawn, as the defense cannot be strengthened. White's Pawn position is so awkward that his King cannot serve any useful defensive purpose.

Thus, if 23 K—K 2, P × P; 24 B × P, B × B; 25 Kt × B, Kt × P ch!; and Black has won his Pawn.

23.	P × P?	... ...

Rendered desperate by the unrelenting pressure, White tries a last "swindle."

23.	... ...	R × R
24.	R × R	R × R
25.	P—B 6	... ...

Naively hoping for 25 ... B ×·B??; 26 P—B 7 and the Pawn must queen. But Black refuses to be taken in.

25.	... ...	R—Q 1
Resigns		

A most instructive example of how to keep up the pressure on weak Pawns.

SUMMARY: White adopted an unsatisfactory opening which gave him a tardy, inharmonious development and an unwieldy Pawn structure. Troublesome Pawn weaknesses soon turned up in his position. By clever maneuvering with his well-posted pieces, Black obtained a grip on the hostile Pawns which made material loss unavoidable for White.

XIV

How to Attack a Formidable
Pawn Center

So ACCUSTOMED have we become to hearing the virtues of
the powerful Pawn center dinned into our ears, that it
may seem incredible that such a Pawn center can be
vulnerable. The fact is, however, that the mighty center
can become top-heavy with anything less than the best
play.

In the hands of a master, the Pawn center is a weapon
at once massive, many-sided and flexible. It can be used
to smother the enemy by a broad advance, to overrun his
flimsy defenses in brilliant fashion, to serve as a bulwark
which screens a crushing concentration of forces.

In the hands of a tyro, an equally imposing center may
turn out to be a colossus—unwieldy, easily exposed to
attack, open to sharp thrusts by fianchettoed Bishops on
the wings. As in the matter of whose ox is gored, the Pawn
center can often turn out to be a highly subjective proposi-
tion.

This has become specially apparent since the revolutionary trends in chess theory which became current about 1920. For centuries, the classical Pawn center (King Pawn and Queen Pawn on the fourth rank) had been deemed the beau ideal of a desirable development. But the Hypermoderns, as the iconoclasts of the Twenties were somewhat ironically called, delighted in taking a topsy-turvy view of the matter, arguing that the "strong" center was really "weak" because it was vulnerable to well-directed counterblows.

Since that time we have learned a great deal about center Pawn formations, and many of the extremes on both sides of the once shrill controversy have canceled out. Present-day theory holds that the classical Pawn center is likely to be very strong, unless the opponent has exceptionally good development at his disposal. The borderline between "strong" and "weak" center is often hard to establish: a "strong" center may become a "weak" center in one move because that move happens to be a pretty feeble one.

The lesson to be learned from this discussion and from the following game is that the center is only as strong as good play by its possessor can make it and keep it so. The player who hopes to demolish the hostile center must try to establish *lasting* pressure. Ephemeral counterattacks which can be brushed off fairly effortlessly, will not serve to make any impression on a sound Pawn center.

GRUENFELD DEFENSE

White	Black
1. P—Q 4	Kt—K B 3
2. P—Q B 4	... ...

So far the play has proceeded as in the eleventh game (page 138), but now Black tries a different tack.

    2. ... ...   **P—K Kt 3**

In the earlier game Black fought for control of White's K 4 square. Here Black indicates from the start that he will make White a present of that vital square—to what end? It all seems very puzzling.

    3. Kt—Q B 3   **P—Q 4**

Diagram 94

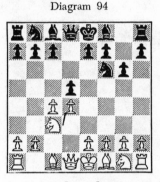

A puzzling defense

Black's last move seems inconsistent. Has he changed his mind after all? Is he going to fight for control of the center? But White sees an easy way to set up an imposing Pawn center:

    4. P × P   ... ...

This dissolves Black's hold on the center—at least as far as Pawn control is concerned.

    4. ... ...   **Kt × P**
    5. P—K 4   ... ...

White has achieved the classical Pawn center—and with gain of time at that.

5. ... ...   Kt × Kt

And Black is very obliging: he exchanges Knights so that White can recapture and give his Queen Pawn powerful Pawn support.

6. P × Kt   P—Q B 4!

Diagram 95

White's center is under fire

Only after Black's last move do we begin to see the method in his madness. White's center is to be under heavy pressure from the King Bishop which Black plans to fianchetto. Meanwhile, Black has already stabbed at the center from the other direction as well.

Now, for the first time in this game, White realizes that he has problems. Of course it would be absurd to ruin his fine Pawn center with 7 P × P?, leaving him with a sickly doubled Pawn in place of the imposing Pawn center he now has. And 7 P—Q 5, while a much better move, still has the drawback of giving Black's King Bishop a magnificent diagonal after 7 ... B—Kt 2.

These sobering considerations help White to conclude that his wisest course will be to leave the center intact, and to protect it with aggressive developing moves. Both adjectives matter: his development must be aggressive *and* protective. If his development is aggressive without being protective, his center Pawns will become wobbly; if his development is protective without being aggressive, Black will develop comfortably, unhampered by any serious problems.

7. B—Q B 4   ... ...

A beautiful square for the Bishop, with an aggressive diagonal aiming at Black's K B 2 square.

7. ... ...   B—Kt 2

The indicated development. Black actually has the effrontery to be threatening to win a Pawn! For White to reply 8 P—K 5 would be poor play on a number of counts: it would commit him to a definite center Pawn formation, limiting his choice of later plans; it would leave him with a backward Queen Pawn, a lasting positional weakness; it would decrease the scope of his Queen Bishop and de-grade it to the purely defensive function of guarding the Queen Pawn.

If Black has achieved nothing else, he has given White plenty to think about on the subject of keeping his center intact.

(*See Diagram 96*)

8. Kt—K 2!   ... ...

Diagram 96

White finds the ideal Knight move

This move allows White to preserve the elasticity of his position; it is admirably protective because it guards the Queen Pawn without subjecting White to a possible pin (as would eventually be the case after 8 Kt—B 3); it is also aggressive, because it allows for such moves as P—K B 4 or B—B 4 or Kt—B 4 at a later stage.

8.   ... ...   Kt—B 3

A good developing move which puts additional pressure on White's Queen Pawn. Once more this Pawn is in need of additional protection. It must be admitted that Black is making out a better case against the impressive Pawn center than might have been expected.

9.   B—K 3   ... ...

Again a developing move which is both protective and aggressive: protective because it guards the Queen Pawn, aggressive because it threatens P—Q 5 most effectively.

9.   ... ...   P × P

The exchange of Pawns is no longer avoidable; it has plus and minus features for both sides.

10.   P × P   ... ...

Diagram 97

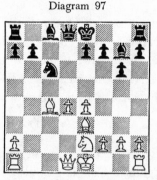

Is White's center strong or weak?

The exchange of Pawns has certainly sharpened the conflict. White's Queen Pawn no longer has Pawn protection and is now dependent more than ever on guardianship by the pieces. If Black can move his Queen and (after castling) play ... R—Q 1, White's center will be under really severe pressure.

But White has made gains as well. The Queen Bishop file is now available for his Rooks, which makes it difficult for Black to find a good square for his Queen. (Prior to the exchange of Pawns, Black had a good spot for his Queen at his Q B 2 square.)

Black has one potential advantage which does not play much of a role now, but may later on: he has two Pawns to one on the Queen-side. In an endgame this may net him a distant passed Pawn with very favorable prospects.

10.   ... ...   **Castles**

Courageously heading for the most difficult variation. The alternative 10 ... Q—R 4 ch; 11 B—Q 2 followed by 12 B—B 3 is unsatisfactory for Black.

11.   Q R—Kt 1   ... ...

White wants to unpin his Queen Pawn along the diagonal, so that he can play P—Q 5 in certain eventualities.

But 11 Castles, is somewhat more exact, as then 11 ... Q—B 2 is answered in that case by 12 R—B 1, preventing 12 ... Kt × P?? because of 13 B × P ch winning the Queen!

11.   ... ...   Q—B 2

Threatening 12 ... Kt × P because of the attack on the Bishop. Black's gain of time is impressively clever, except that White's reply is impressive by reason of its very simplicity!

12.   Castles   ... ...

The point is that after 12 ... Kt × P; White plays 13 B × P ch, followed by 14 B × Kt, remaining with the preferable Pawn position because of Black's isolated King Pawn.

12.   ... ...   R—Q 1

The critical point. Black has attained the maximum pressure against White's Pawn center, and it must be admitted that he has made out a good case.

(*See Diagram 98*)

Black has marshaled his forces against the Queen Pawn very effectively. White's center looks shaky indeed (if 13 P—K 5?, Kt × K P), but 13 R—B 1 keeps up the fight (if

Diagram 98

Triple attack on White's Queen Pawn

---

then 13 ... Kt × Q P??; 14 B × P ch winning Black's
Queen).

13. P—Q 5   ... ...

White loses patience in the face of the pitiless pressure
applied against his Queen Pawn. But now Black revives
his attack on the center.

13. ... ...   **P—K 3!**

Well played. Black insists on demonstrating that the
Queen Pawn is weak, wherever it is. At this point White's
position is very critical.

14. Q—B 1?   ... ...

Weak. Only with 14 Kt—B 4 could White have justified
hopes of holding the position.

(*See Diagram 99*)

14. ... ...   **Kt—R 4!**

This is the move that White missed. His center is de-
molished at the cost of a Pawn.

Diagram 99

Black smashes the Pawn center

---

15. B—Kt 3   ... ...

Much worse is the spasmodic defensive move 15 R—
Kt 4?, which is met by 15 ... B—B 1.

15.	**Q × Q**
16. K R × Q	**Kt × B**
17. R × Kt	**P × P**

Black has won the Pawn, but as he is considerably behind in development, he has some trouble making his
material advantage stick.

18. R—Q 1   **B—K 3**

(See Diagram 100)

The most plausible course here for White is 19 R × Kt P.
But after 19 ... P × P; 20 R × R ch, R × R; Black
threatens ... R—Q 8 mate, which gives him time to maintain his material advantage.

19. R/Kt 3—Q 3   ... ...

Diagram 100

White cannot reestablish material equality

This intensification of the pin looks promising, But Black has a way out.

19. ... ...   P—Q 5!

Nicely played. If 20 B × P?, B—B 5! wins for Black. Or if 20 Kt × P, B × P; and Black his two connected passed Pawns on the Queen-side which will win easily for him.

20. Kt—B 1   K R—Q B 1

Black returns the extra Pawn temporarily, as he finds the pin too uncomfortable.

21. B × P   B × B
22. R × B   R—B 7

This occupation of the seventh rank is very powerful, for example 23 P—Q R 4, R/R 1—Q B 1; 24 Kt—Q 3, R/B 1—B 5; and White is without good moves, the loss of a Pawn being unavoidable.

23. R/Q 4—Q 2   R/R 1—Q B 1

Threatening 24 ... R × R or 24 ... R × Kt. White is helpless.

	24. R × R	R × R

And now White can no longer stave off material loss (25
P—Q R 3, R—B 6; or 25 P—Q R 4, R—B 5).

	25. K—B 1	B × P

With two connected passed Pawns on the Queen-side,
Black has an easy win.

26.	Kt × B	R × Kt
27.	R—Q 7	P—Q Kt 4
28.	K—K 1	P—Kt 5

Resigns

Further play would be pointless, in view of the power of
the passed Pawns.

SUMMARY: After an opening in which Black willingly
permitted his opponent to build a strong Pawn center,
Black consistently brought pressure to bear on White's
Queen Pawn. White failed to find the best ways of maintaining his center, and his position collapsed with surprising suddenness.

Index

Other books in the acclaimed MACMILLAN CHESS LIBRARY are available at your local bookstore or by mail. To order directly, return the coupon below to: Macmillan Publishing Company Special Sales Department, 866 Third Avenue, New York, N.Y. 10022.

ISBN	TITLE/AUTHOR	PRICE	QUANTITY
0020114907	CARO-KANN: CLASSICAL 4 . . . Bf5 (Kasparov/Shakarov)	$8.95	_____
0020117604	FROM BEGINNER TO EXPERT IN 40 LESSONS (Kostyev/Speelman)	8.95	_____
0020114303	GRAND PRIX ATTACK (Hodgson/Day)	8.95	_____
0020288905	HOW TO IMPROVE YOUR CHESS (Horowitz)	8.95	_____
0020114206	HOW TO LEARN FROM YOUR DEFEATS (Karpov)	8.95	_____
0020290802	IMPROVE YOUR CHESS RESULTS (Zak)	8.95	_____
0020287208	MANEUVERS IN MOSCOW (Keene/ Goodman)	8.95	_____
0025541404	MACMILLAN HANDBOOK OF CHESS (Horowitz)	12.95	_____
0020114109	MINIATURES FROM THE WORLD CHAMPIONS (Karpov)	8.95	_____
0020297704	MORPHY CHESS MASTERPIECES (Reinfeld)	2.95	_____
0020290500	THE OFFICIAL LAWS OF CHESS (Kazic) Available July 1986	10.95	_____
0020282702	OPEN GAMBITS (Botterill) Available July 1986	8.95	_____
0020119801	PLAYING CHESS (Wade)	8.95	_____
0020290209	SPANISH GAMBITS (Shankovich) Available July 1986	8.95	_____
0020290608	SPANISH . . . WITHOUT a6 (Yudovich) Available July 1986	8.95	_____
0020297203	CHESS MASTERS ON WINNING CHESS (Reinfeld)	3.95	_____
0020297602	WINNING CHESS OPENINGS (Reinfeld)	7.95	_____

Sub-Total _____
Please add postage and handling costs—$1.00 for the first book
and 50¢ for each additional book _____
Sales tax—if applicable _____
TOTAL _____

_____ Enclosed is my check/money order payable to Macmillan Publishing Company
_____ Bill My _____ MasterCard _____ Visa / Card # _____
Expiration date _____ Signature _____
—Charge orders valid only with signature—

Lines   Units

Control No.   T-Code

Account Number/San _____   For charge orders only:

Ship to: _____   Bill to: _____

_____   _____

_____ Zip Code   _____ Zip Code

For discount information regarding bulk purchases please write to Special Sales Director at the above address. Publisher's prices are subject to change without notice. Offer good January 1, 1986 through December 31, 1986. Allow 3 weeks for delivery.

FC# _____